Additional Praise for
Advisory Leadership

"In the 20 years that I have known Greg, I have rarely met a more consummate professional; he is a true credit to his profession. The wisdom he shares in his book is not to be missed."

—Thomas D. Giachetti, Esq., Chairman, Securities Practice Group, Stark & Stark

"If culture is 'what happens when no one is watching,' Greg Friedman's book gives the owners and leaders of advisory businesses a detailed and very practical guide to making sure that the right things happen in their firms. The value of the book comes from not just its thorough treatment of the subject but also the practicality of the advice—Greg continues to lead one of the premier firms in the industry and he has the 'battle scars' to prove it."

—Philip Palaveev, CEO, The Ensemble Practice, LLC, and industry consultant

"*Advisory Leadership* provides great advice with real-life action steps for any business. It is an excellent book for business leaders."

—Dan Skiles, President, Shareholders Service Group

"Greg is a successful entrepreneur who has been sharing his experiences and offering advice to the advisory industry for many years. As a colleague and friend, I am excited that Greg has formalized his teachings in this amazing book. His straightforward advice is easy to absorb, and each chapter is full of practical strategies and tactics that can be implemented simply and will have an immediate impact on your business."

—Kelli Cruz, Founder, Cruz Consulting Group

Advisory Leadership

Using the Seven Steps of Heart Culture to Create Lasting Success for Any Wealth Management Firm

Gregory H. Friedman

WILEY

Cover image: © iStock.com/Rapid Eye
Cover design: Wiley

Published by John Wiley & Sons, Inc., Hoboken, New Jersey.
Published simultaneously in Canada.

For general information on our other products and services or for technical support,
please contact our Customer Care Department within the United States at (800) 762-
2974, outside the United States at (317) 572-3993 or fax (317) 572-4002.

Wiley publishes in a variety of print and electronic formats and by print-on-demand.
Some material included with standard print versions of this book may not be included
in e-books or in print-on-demand. If this book refers to media such as a CD or DVD
that is not included in the version you purchased, you may download this material
at http://booksupport.wiley.com. For more information about Wiley products, visit
www.wiley.com.

ISBN 978-1-119-13608-8 (Hardcover)
ISBN 978-1-119-13610-1 (ePDF)
ISBN 978-1-119-13609-5 (ePub)

Printed in the United States of America

10 9 8 7 6 5 4 3 2 1

*This book is dedicated to my mother, Eleanor Duemling,
and my father, (the late) C. Hugh Friedman.*

Contents

Foreword

G reg Friedman is one big walking heart. Don't let that fool you; he successfully leads with it. So many of us in business mistake leadership for power and forcefulness. The very nature of the word conjures up a powerful figure: standing, arms forward, commanding the pack. Greg reminds us it's possible to lead while standing beside, or even behind, those who look to you for authority and guidance.

One of the great things about aging is that you genuinely can't remember when you became friends with people, but it often seems like you have known them forever. I don't know the year that I met Greg, but I vividly remember the circumstances around it. My partner and I had just spent a small fortune paying a programmer to create client relationship management software that we could use to track client-related work and to keep a diary of our relationship with our clients. There was nothing like this on the market and we sorely needed it. Heck, the whole industry needed it. But our results were a disaster.

Then I heard that Greg and his partner, Ken Golding, had just created something that might really work. I picked up the phone to ask him about it. I told him what a mess we'd created. I told him how much money we had thrown away on our project. And I told him that I had no idea where to go next. Greg didn't wait a heartbeat to offer assistance. "Look," he said, "we've got something we call BAM (basically a monkey can do it). I'll give it to you. All I ask is that if you have some good suggestions about what we could do to make it better, share them with me." Greg's passion for creating a better work product to support all advisors, not just his firm, is definitely leading with heart.

Through the years Greg and I spent many conferences skipping presentations and sitting together to share ideas, experiences, and philosophies. As Greg talked about his family, his clients, and his staff, it was clear that his leadership style rested squarely in creating personal growth and satisfaction for everyone with whom he came in contact. He's a great listener, and he puts what he hears into positive action. More important, he is very eager to share his cultural leadership tenets of employing patience, honesty, integrity, compassion, respect, persistence, consistency, encouragement, and courage; all of these helped him create success in not just one, but two separate businesses.

I think you'll find yourself in this book. You'll recognize some leadership habits you'd like to jettison and discover new ones that feel as comfortable as slipping on an old, well-worn sweater. I know you'll enjoy Greg's writing style.

It's relaxed, satisfying, and enjoyable, much like sitting down and having a good conversation with the man himself. You'll realize how easy it is to adapt your leadership style to your natural tendencies, not just to some "make it so" book that outlines how a great leader should think and act. You'll walk through his process of cultural transition and change, recognizing how leading with heart promotes a happy, healthy—and yes, profitable—working environment. Enjoy.

Deena Katz, CFP®, LHD
Associate Professor, Department of Personal Financial
Planning, Texas Tech University;
Founding Partner, Evensky & Katz Wealth Management;
Author of seven books on financial planning and practice
management topics

Preface

What is it worth as a leader to have a successful and thriving company? Does the value of a firm increase with employees who are motivated and inspired, who enjoy working together and who find coming to work every day rewarding and challenging?

What may sound like an unrealistic ideal is actually an attainable feat if you focus on an element of your business that you may have overlooked—your firm's culture.

Historically leaders have analyzed how they can better engage employees, focusing primarily on the success of the firm. In today's landscape, truly meaningful leadership must go a step further, flipping yesteryear's notions of *firm first* thinking and instead doing something that should come naturally to all of us: Putting people first.

If that sounds precarious, consider the facts about our industry. The wealth management space is on the cusp of monumental change in its life cycle, with a large number of advisors looking ahead at succession planning and retirement. The next generation of advisors—your firm's successors—have different values and priorities than their predecessors. Your next clients, the Gen X and Gen Y contingent, also have different (and some would argue higher) expectations of their advisors than their parents do. Technology is abundant and data is accessible in one click. Instant gratification is a foregone conclusion. What does this all mean?

The only thing that truly separates and elevates your firm is your people.

In *Advisory Leadership*, you'll learn how seven key steps can help you transform your firm's culture, including, if necessary, how to reverse the course of your current culture to create a dynamic, energetic environment of happy, engaged employees. These seven steps, based on human virtues we all strive to achieve, are the key to unlocking the power of a people-first culture:

1. **Patience.** Slowing down the hiring process to help the firm better choose the right candidate for any role, every time.
2. **Honesty and Integrity.** Leading by example and encouraging open and honest communication.
3. **Compassion.** Acknowledging people for their individual contributions and getting to know them beyond their roles.
4. **Respect.** Empowering employees to make decisions and guiding them in their personal goals for professional achievement.

5. **Persistence and Consistency.** Aligning your management team with your firm's goals and reiterating your values through various communication channels.
6. **Encouragement.** Promoting and rewarding team collaboration instead of competition.
7. **Courage.** Looking inward before taking those crucial first steps toward change.

This book will cover each of these steps in its own dedicated chapter, and provide actionable tips at the end to help you get started on your own path to creating a healthy and thriving company culture. It will also cover how to make lasting, positive changes that encourage your team to help protect and promote your values.

Along the way, you'll also find interesting real-world examples of heart culture elevating a firm's success as well as some pitfalls to sidestep, which are based on my own experiences in the advisory business.

For principals, advisors, and team leaders in the wealth management industry, you'll recognize many of the common challenges we face in our unique environment. And though the title is *Advisory Leadership*, many of the principles in this book can be applied to anyone who is trying to run a successful business.

If like me you got into this business to help people, you'll find that many of the messages in this book will seem like common sense.

Listening.
Being honest.
Caring.
Getting to know people.
Encouraging them to succeed.

We are in the service business, after all, and our job is to learn as much as possible about our clients in order to help them achieve their financial and life goals. We're good at it. These seven steps succeed in using those same innate skills we have as advisors and as people to help us build a stronger, more cohesive team with shared goals and a shared philosophy of how we work, how we deliver financial advice, and what we want to achieve personally as well as professionally.

Ultimately a leader wants to build a thriving, fulfilling business by using the best tools and resources available to become more profitable and to reach more clients. Consider *Advisory Leadership* one of those resources: A tool to help you unlock your business's potential and to cultivate your firm's most valuable resource—your people.

Acknowledgments

This book was inspired by many people, and without their encouragement and support—and life lessons—it would not have happened. I want to thank in particular Deena Katz for being a relentless advocate for our industry and for her staunch encouragement to write this book.

I am grateful to all of the many people I have worked with over my career—both professionally and personally—who helped shape who I am as a leader, who I've learned from, and whom I consider my friends. In particular I want to thank Ken Golding, Dan Skiles, John Shangler, Jim Herrington, Mark Tibergien, Susan Dickson, Tim Welsh, Philip Palaveev, Harold Evensky, Tom Giachetti, Marion Asnes, Jamie Green, Larry Ginsburg, Erin Kincheloe, Colin Drake, Cynthia Greenfield, Jim Placak, Bill Burke, Sharon Hoover, Kerry Elkind, and so many more amazing friends and colleagues in our industry who have taught me valuable lessons and been a tremendous support.

An immense amount of credit is due to the people along the way who helped inspire and educate me over the years, and to them I would like to express my gratitude for their continued support and their friendship. A strong, successful culture begins with relationships and grows as you build trust, encourage growth, and share new ideas. I thank each and every employee I have worked with in the past (and will work with in the future) at Junxure and Private Ocean for working with me to create great things—I believe together we have made a difference!

And of course I am so grateful for my family—my wife, Laurie, and my twins, Andrew and Marissa—who keep me grounded and teach me every day!

Introduction

Understanding Heart Culture

Making the Change

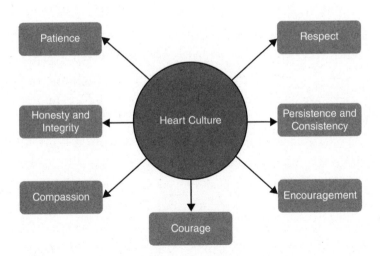

A ll business leaders share a common goal—to inspire their employees and to see profitable results in the business. That inspiration then encourages collaboration, which leads to success. In today's evolving business environment—and in the financial services industry especially—a successful and balanced corporate culture begins with a leadership mentality that appeals to the heart first and the mind second.

What *is* heart culture? At its core, heart culture symbolizes how a firm values more than just an employee's output. That it's not about the work, but rather, the *people* who do the work. This may seem like simple human nature, but in the business world, heart culture is a rising movement that is quickly supplanting the cold, hard corporate machine of yesteryear. The truth is, leaders can no longer afford to ignore the shift toward a people-first culture and its direct influence on a healthy, effective work environment. Leaders today need to be flexible, fluid, caring, and individualistic to be competitive in today's market.

This book was written not just for financial advisors but for any leader looking to make a sea change in his or her company culture. Many of these lessons, which I learned on my own professional journey as both an employee and a leader, have helped shape my views on successful and fulfilling leadership that leads to employee retention and company growth. In fact, another key benefit of creating a heart culture is that you will attract talent.

I have been a financial advisor for more than 25 years and am currently the president and CEO of Private Ocean, a wealth management firm in the San Francisco Bay Area that is the product of a merger of my firm, Friedman & Associates, with Salient Wealth Management. I am also the cofounder and president of Junxure, a technology firm based in Raleigh, North Carolina, that provides customer relationship management (CRM) and office management solutions to financial advisors.

My career—like many of our industry leaders—sprang from humble beginnings. In high school I started working part time for a warehouse retail chain stocking shelves, and after a decade I had worked my way up the ladder of that company while finishing college and graduate school. I did many jobs in that company—from driving a forklift to sales to accounting and purchasing. I learned a lot in those years, including the value of loyalty.

What I also experienced during that time was a spectrum of different kinds of leaders that truly covered a gamut of styles. It helped shape the kind of leader I wanted to be, and I made a conscious effort early on to treat people differently than I was treated on many occasions. I always knew I wanted to have my own business, and that I wanted to do things differently from the norm—certainly differently from what I experienced.

What follows are Seven Steps of Heart Culture—human values—that are vital to making a difference in a firm's culture and in a leader's influence within that firm.

These seven steps also represent the life cycle of a healthy relationship between a leader and an employee. From the hiring process—immeasurably important to building a culture—to maintenance and growth, each phase has its own set of challenges and rewards that can either hinder a firm's growth or help it soar to new levels.

This book focuses on each of these seven key interconnected elements of creating *and maintaining* a heart culture. I have learned that being good at one or two of the ideas, or focusing on different ones at different times over the year or years, doesn't lead to a sustainable heart culture. In reality, I have found it's better to aspire to all seven even if I cannot be great at all of them at any given time!

Over the next seven chapters I will go into detail about each of these steps. I will also share stories of personal successes and missteps in developing the leadership style that has proven very effective in my businesses. At the end of each chapter I have included some practical, real-world tips that you can use to get started on your own path to successful and fulfilling leadership.

Now, as with every journey, we will begin by taking the first step.

Chapter 1

Patience

Taking Your Time to Find the Right People

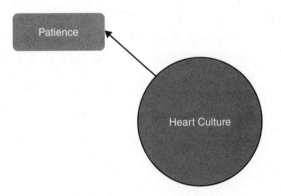

O ne of the questions I am asked most often in my position is how I manage two companies on two coasts. I always respond in the same way.

It's all about the people around me. I am surrounded by great, quality people who work hard and are as passionate about the work we do as I am. For me, that means working longer hours and racking up lots of frequent flier miles. But the payoff is worth the time and jet lag. Why? Because the culture that's been established in both companies moves both ships forward and that creates success and growth.

That culture, which is very similar in both companies, is based on caring, respect, empowerment, collaboration, and a powerful sense of team. There is also a clear, and common, sense of purpose and mission in both companies.

That sense of team serves as the foundation that drives us forward, weathering growing pains and a changing industry toward innovation and profitability.

What we have accomplished in our culture—and I say "we" because credit is due to all of the people I am fortunate enough to work with—is not only potent, it's game changing for companies that struggle to create a cohesive team in corporate environments today.

Employee loyalty and satisfaction are at the core of building *heart culture*, and it should come as no surprise that creating and cultivating this type of environment begins in the hiring process.

The first element of heart leadership is patience, and it is vital for leaders to exercise self-discipline during the recruitment, interview, and hiring process if they want to protect the integrity of the firm's culture.

Before we get started, though, I'd like to share some truths about my personal leadership style.

Since the beginning of my career I have known that I wanted diversity of thought and collaboration. I wanted different voices. I wanted ideas. Also, I wanted to build a happy and healthy environment that people wanted to come to five days a week. What I did not want was to be a leader who was overcontrolling and commanding.

That desire to help others achieve happiness in their work and in their lives is a foundational part of how I lead and how I encourage others to lead. With new hires, setting expectations on day one (and even earlier in the interview process) helps determine whether a particular candidate is the right fit for my firm.

For example, when new employees come on board at one of my companies, I start with the same conversation that I have had for many years.

At Private Ocean, for example, I talk to them about our philosophy, our purpose, and our culture, and what we want to achieve as a whole. I talk about my personal mission—what drives me—and the company mission. I want to make sure we're on the same page when it comes to financial planning and wealth management and how to take care of clients. For us, financial planning should be objective and focused on helping people achieve their life goals—what's important to *them* in their lives. Financial planning and investments are just the tools we use. Making sure potential candidates share the same philosophies that guide basic priorities of the company is the first thing I like to nail down.

Then I give them my "I Have a Dream" speech, in which I acknowledge that if all of us had unlimited money and resources we would likely be on a tropical island someplace, sitting in a hammock on the beach and watching the world pass by, or engaged in philanthropy.

I tell them that I understand that the primary reason most of us work is because we have to. Everyone has bills to pay and, most likely, families to support. But aside from money, my dream is that when an employee wakes up and puts her feet on the ground, she's excited about going to a cool place to work, doing cool things with cool people, and working with cool clients.

Appealing to people's emotional connection with and pride in what they do is one of the keys to unlocking heart culture. Whether they're passionate about coaching their daughter's soccer games, traveling the world, or—in our industry—helping people achieve their financial goals, the result of inspiration is the same. People invest more of themselves in something they believe in and are passionate about. Get a group of these people in one place working toward the same goal, and a business can reach new heights.

PERSPECTIVE: SAVING WHALES

If you were faced with the job of stuffing a thousand envelopes and then hauling them to the post office to be stamped and mailed, you could view it as a repetitive, boring, and menial task. Some would argue that they're too skilled or too educated to do that type of thing. But what if you were stuffing envelopes for a cause you were passionate about? What if you were saving whales, or, in our industry, fostering better client relationships and offering higher-level service?

One person may say with a heavy sigh, "I'm too talented to do this," while another would say with great enthusiasm, "I'm saving whales!" No matter the task at hand, it's always about perspective. It's a leader's job to identify this perspective and passion in the hiring process, and foster an attitude that reminds employees that what they do is for the greater good of the firm and their clients. Their work has a higher purpose!

Now if that approach described in the previous Saving Whales sidebar seems a bit of a reach for leaders (and especially advisors) to grasp, consider this: The financial industry today is in a state of transition, with the average age of advisors rising (mid-50s and up) and the available pool of talented young financial planners struggling to keep up with demand. Part of a leader's job is to adapt to this evolution and recognize that new hires have very different values from their parents. What I have found in both my companies is that heart leadership—and heart culture—really resonates with Next Gen employees.

Next Gen Employees: Changing Values, Changing Culture

In the past 10 years, culture has played a growing part (and often is the deciding factor) in younger candidates' search for a firm that aligns with their goals and values.

What's changed from the past? Everything! Although you may have said to yourself that you'd never give the "In my day . . ." speech that you heard from your parents, you may catch yourself saying that you didn't have the Internet when you were growing up, or that texting was passing notes in science class. What's iOS? What's Wi-Fi? You tell your children, "In my day, you took the job you were given at the rate they were willing to pay, you put in 60 hours a week, you took one vacation a year, and you were grateful!"

All kidding aside, employees today have different priorities from previous generations, including a higher value placed on work/life balance, stress-relieving activities, and even a passion for social consciousness and community engagement. In some instances vacation and paid time off are worth as much or more than a higher salary, and flexible schedules that give employees more remote options are considered far more attractive than a corner office. Some truly forward-thinking firms throw in additional perks that were unheard of years ago—job sharing to learn new skills, flexible project assignments, gym facilities, paid time off for volunteer work, and educational reimbursement—to help sweeten the deal. Most of all, firms are less and less committed to confining employees to a set job description and instead give employees the ability to think outside of their defined roles.

Taking Your Time during the Hiring Process

As advisors, it's important to consider what we're up against when it comes to attracting new hires. Recruiting for the best new planners (and any other position in a firm) these days is like lacing up the gloves for a title bout. The talent shortage has heightened the level of competitiveness across our industry, and it's crucial to find a way to separate your firm from the pack. That's why now the differentiator for many firms is their level of commitment to client service. In my firms, one of the major components of choosing the right employee is finding someone who shares our philosophy of taking great care of clients—both internal and external. The competition is fierce, and with so many advisors interested in succession planning, there's definitely an urgency in fighting for those candidates who look best on paper.

But that's a problem if you're looking to build heart culture. A candidate with a stellar résumé does not automatically translate to a stellar addition to your firm. Finding the right person takes time and patience, which cannot and should not be cut short for the sake of winning a race. In both of my companies we go through an extended hiring process that is key to creating the right team.

What are the benefits to investing time in a longer hiring process? If you have one formal conversation with someone for an hour, you'll likely get plenty of rehearsed answers—anyone can be up for "game time" for an interview or two. But if you have several conversations with different groups of employees in different settings, you'll get a much more complete picture of candidates. Do they communicate well with different teams? Do they share the same passion for what they'll be expected to do? Are they team players? What do they want to achieve in their personal and professional lives over the long term? Who *are* they?

Taking your time during the hiring process means that you'll be much more likely to choose someone who has an understanding of expectations, shares your business philosophy, feels his ideas will be heard, and is excited to be on board. Those qualities lead to lower turnover and the fostering of greater loyalty over time. The way we explain it to candidates: It is to *their* advantage to be learning more about us and the work.

Four Steps to Hiring the Right Candidate

The hiring process can be daunting, and firms may be tempted to choose an applicant based on impressive credentials rather than finding a cultural fit. These steps can help guide you in your search for the right candidate.

1. **Hold lots of interviews with lots of people.** You're doing your company a disservice if you choose a new hire based only on numbers or Ivy League credentials. Many times I have found the most suitable candidate is someone who has less experience but more passion for the work. In a handful of cases, these people have been career changers who became game changers—people who changed completely from their previous professions to try something they've always wanted to do.

   I recommend scheduling a series of interviews—one with a direct manager and then additional in-person meet-and-greets with the people this candidate would be working with day in and day out. It does not matter how qualified someone may seem on paper. Observing how she engages with different groups of people can provide meaningful insight—you learn motivations, passions, and personality traits—and you can quickly tell if this person fits (or does not fit) in your environment.

At both my companies I interview everybody at some point. Exactly *where* in the process I get involved depends on the role, but in general I begin early in the hiring process and then return at the end, once the team has collectively decided on its preferred candidates. For example, for advisor candidates, I am always involved early in the interview process and play a part until the end when we make a hiring decision. These are roles that involve working heavily with clients and directly reflect upon the firm's culture and philosophy of wealth management. In other areas of the company, such as client services, I leave the initial screenings up to the people with the most expertise. Are the candidates a good fit with the team? Do they seem to share our philosophy? Would they be assets to the firm? How does one candidate excel over another? I leave these discussions up to the team and then meet with the candidates who meet the group's highest standards.

In the technology firm my involvement in the hiring process is primarily associated with leadership roles. I rely on these people to ensure the ongoing health of our success and our culture, so it's crucial to me to have the right people leading the team. For every other role in the firm, I leave the hiring decisions up to leadership and to those with relatively more experience with the role. These are mainly technical positions, and trusting those you hire to make decisions is part of taking your time in finding the right people to put in charge. In these situations the right hire is more about finding someone who is a cultural fit for the firm.

In both firms there isn't a formal protocol for the interview process, but it's important to stay organized. We typically start with a phone screening by our human resources manager and then set up face-to-face meetings with team leads, different teams, and small groups to change up the dynamics. From there we may do an off-site lunch to see the candidate in a different environment, where he may let his guard down. These meetings are unrehearsed and the setting unfamiliar (unlike a normal conference room setting), which gives us great insight into the candidate and helps us to determine if there is a natural chemistry within the team.

Some have joked that interviewing for one of my firms is a bit like boot camp for candidates, but once we explain our process and that its purpose is for them to look at us also, everyone, especially the right people, appreciate the time we take to get to know them to ensure that this is truly a good fit for all parties.

2. **Choose your questions wisely.** Are the candidates as focused on your priorities as you are, or do they just want to work an eight-to-five job and enjoy a short commute? How passionate are they about client service? What are they looking to get out of the position in question? What motivates them? What are they passionate about? You can teach skill, but you cannot teach heart. Ask the questions that you'd want someone to ask you if you were the candidate. Also, encourage the candidates to ask

questions about the firm. Their questions can be as revealing as their answers.

FIVE KEY INTERVIEW QUESTIONS

By the time I interview candidates they've likely met a handful or more of people regarding the position. I assume the typical questions have been covered, so I focus more on trying to see if the person is a cultural fit for the firm. Here are a few questions I pose to potential new hires:

1. **What motivates you?** A developer I hired recently answered this question by saying that he "just loved working on cool technology," and that he liked what we were working on. It got him excited to be innovative, and that's exactly what we wanted, not only for the role but also for the company. Wouldn't you want to work with someone who was excited to come to work every day?

2. **What are you passionate about?** Hiring isn't just about credentials; there needs to be a connection to the firm's values. And on a human level, gauging people's motivation extends beyond the role and into everything they do. Finding out what people are passionate about and why is a great window into someone's personality.

3. **What are you telling your family/spouse about our company?** This question often

(Continued)

(*Continued*)

takes candidates off guard and results in some rather interesting, and often honest, answers. How they talk about the company to those closest to them says a lot about their motives and their personalities, and in particular how much they want to join the firm.

4. **What did you enjoy most/find most challenging in your last position?** These responses give you a glimpse into what people enjoy most about their work as well as what might be difficult for them to manage. There are no right or wrong answers, necessarily. This question is a great assessment of the candidate, especially when considering certain roles.

5. **What opportunities do you see for yourself here?** In my companies there is great diversity of personality. What everyone has in common is great passion for what they do, for the people they call clients, and for working together to achieve success. They're also in it for the long haul. Finding out how people see themselves growing within the firm is very encouraging and opens the door to many possibilities.

3. **Understand their values and motives.** Younger generation planners and employees today don't necessarily have the same values, beliefs, and goals as their parents, but one thing is clear: They are passionate about making a difference and helping people. The

perks I mentioned earlier that have become more commonplace—job sharing, paid time off for volunteer work, and so on—are just some of the examples of how much has changed.

YOU CAN TEACH SKILL, BUT YOU CAN'T TEACH HEART

During the hiring process I often tell candidates that by the time they come in for their interviews we already know that they're qualified for the positions they have applied for. That qualification may not mean they have the highest credentials or the most impressive résumés, but it does mean that they have the potential to grow. What we want to teach them, we are confident they can learn. But what we can't teach them is to have passion for taking great care of clients, doing excellent work, and having pride in their work ethic and respect for their fellow employees.

---

4. **Change the scenery.** A longer interview process can start to seem like a police interrogation if you don't change things up. To avoid questions becoming repetitive and responses becoming stale or formulaic, be sure to set interviews with different groups in different locations. Have the candidate visit several times, meeting with different people in your firm as well as in different locations. Have lunch and watch the way they interact and behave, and also put them

in situations that they will be in if hired—and observe. While I know that's not a new practice, it's important to consider the venue as part of the interview. See how candidates interact with the servers and how they conduct themselves in a more social environment. It's at the lunch—or after several visits—that people start to get comfortable and show their true colors.

At the end of the interview cycle, work with the different parts of your team to compare notes and give feedback. You may find that a candidate makes a great impression on his potential managers, but a not so great one on colleagues.

ADVICE FOR GROWING FIRMS

A longer hiring process, particularly when you're just starting out in the financial services business, can be challenging. The reality is, patience isn't a virtue you can necessarily afford day in and day out. You have to grow. You need to get established so that success will build on itself. The sooner and faster you can get a few clients in the door, the sooner you'll get more momentum.

But the one area that you have to stand still in long enough to assess is choosing the people you want to join you and help you on your journey. You may not have the luxury of being patient, but you must make time to hire the right people.

I recommend defining what success looks like to you and your firm. Do you want to grow rapidly or do you want to become more of a lifestyle firm? Look inward for answers, and understand that with all growth come failures. Overcoming those failures is a lot easier when you've taken the time to build a team that shares your goals and your motivation.

Although there's no foreseeing every pitfall that can derail your hiring plans, one of the most common mistakes that leaders make is hiring someone too quickly.

No matter how diligent you may be in your hiring practices, chances are there has been that one time where you rushed to hire someone. Did you need to fill a critical spot during tax season? Did you need to snag that top advisor before some other firm snatched him or her up? Maybe you bypassed checking all of the references, or you overlooked a few "minor" red flags during the interview process. Red flags can be subtle— anything from not making enough eye contact during an interview to typos on a résumé. Bigger warnings may include sloppiness or lack of communication skills. Did candidates seem confident at the interview or arrogant? If they were rude or dismissive to service people at an off-site lunch interview, would they be well suited for a service culture?

I always tell my team that they should never underestimate the power of their "little voice" during the hiring process. It's important to trust yourself and your instincts about a candidate. You'll find that just as quickly as you drop someone into a key role, you may discover that she just doesn't fit. It can be a costly lesson to learn too late.

Regardless of how badly you need that new position filled, take one step back and consider the cost of *not* taking the time to find someone right for the job. Times are changing for advisors, and to stay competitive you have to evolve.

So while it may seem like time is ticking away during an extended hiring process, it's important to focus on the bigger picture and carefully choose every person that you add to your team. Ask yourself, "Does this candidate share my outlook on client service? Do his long-term goals line up with mine?" Check his references. Study his employment history. Don't be distracted by shiny accolades or accomplishments. Most important, listen to your little voice—if something seems amiss, it probably is! If you've already hired someone who is not meeting expectations, assess the damage; it may be time to roll up your sleeves and see if clear expectations and guidance can help steer him your way. Last, know when to call it—if someone simply is not right for your firm, don't waste time trying to make it work.

What it all comes down to is heart—hiring with heart. You have to care, genuinely care, about the people you serve and how you can improve their lives.

PATIENCE RECAP: TIPS TO REMEMBER

- Hire *slowly*—resist the urge to just fill the position and get it done by hiring the candidate with the best résumé. Take your time!
- Everyone in the firm has a stake in new hires—make sure to gather feedback from as many people as possible.
- Regardless of how badly you need that new position filled, take one step back and consider the cost of *not* taking the time to find someone right for the job.
- Make sure that your hiring process includes a number of meetings, varied locations, and different types of interviews.

Benefits

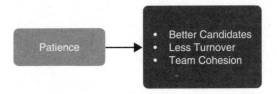

Chapter 2

Honesty and Integrity

Speaking Openly and Walking the Walk

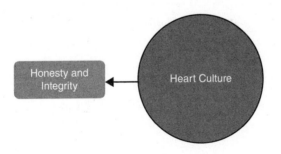

M any business leaders share the perception that the less employees know about the company—such as financial information, internal and external challenges, goals, recruitment efforts, and so on—the better.

The reason, some believe, is that sharing too much undermines confidence in the firm and its leadership.

I believe the opposite is true when it comes to creating heart culture, and I think it takes a great deal of confidence to be open and honest. While some leaders may interpret complete authenticity to equal weakness and vulnerability, what they don't realize is that people—whether it be employees or your clients—appreciate hearing the facts.

Especially in the financial services field, in which market volatility keeps everyone on their guard, it's important for leaders to consider sharing more information than they are used to for the sake of building trust and loyalty.

This philosophy is further supported in the book *Getting Naked: A Business Fable about Shedding the Three Fears That Sabotage Client Loyalty* by Patrick Lencioni.[1] There's a powerful theme there about how being honest with clients and employees encourages confidence and support.

So how can a leader maintain stability while sharing information that may be sensitive or that may not always be positive? It's not as easy as it sounds, but the benefit of sharing as much information as possible means every person in your organization feels included and invested in the firm's well-being.

Overcommunicate Your Values and Philosophy

To nurture a culture that is based on an open communication model, begin by being deliberate and proactive about sharing your values and philosophy within the company.

Your communication should always reinforce your beliefs, therefore setting a standard for employees to use as a guide when interacting with their leaders, their coworkers, and even your clients.

That being said, communication takes many forms, and sometimes getting your point across is less about what you say and more about what you do. I often say when it comes to communicating values, "tell them, tell them again, and then show them."

I start by telling my new hires that my personal values form the basis for what we expect from employees, and that we've already identified these values within the employee through the hiring process. This is the starting point in this new relationship and sets the tone of what the employee should expect to accomplish in his or her role.

I then reiterate the following basic core values:

- **Integrity and ethics.** We start with integrity for two reasons. First, because in the financial planning business your word is your reputation. That reputation is extremely hard to earn and very easy to lose—and at the end of the day it is all you have. Second, Ken Golding and I started Junxure on a handshake and each other's promise to follow through on our word. Or as Ken says, "When you say you're going to do something, do it." Be a person of your word. Always do the right thing for your client, customer, employee, and others—even when it hurts or is at your personal expense.
- **Extreme service.** We work in the client services business, and the client is king. Everything we do is focused on making our clients' lives easier, and good service is not good enough. "Good" and "Okay" are forgettable.

That's why we always strive for a +1 experience—that is, great service plus that something extra that goes above and beyond expectations. I tell my employees to be memorable any time they interact with clients—both external *and* internal clients!

- **Collegiality and a sense of humor.** This value shows up as "don't take yourself too seriously" and "you better have a sense of humor!" It's important in our culture to promote a "work hard, play hard" outlook that conveys our team mentality. Because we do spend a considerable time choosing a new hire, we want her to feel as if she's part of a fun, passionate group of people who all want to achieve the same things.

- **Open and honest communication.** Front and center is our mission to openly communicate with our employees and our clients. This, of course, is always a battle and a continuum, as there are certainly situations that warrant confidentiality. In this respect, the goal is to communicate to employees that they should not just sit on something that's frustrating them or that's become an obstacle to their work. We encourage communication that's respectful and aware of other points of view.

- **Constant and never-ending innovation and improvement (CAN I).** Never settle! In both of my firms we are always asking, "How can I do this differently? How can I do this better for the client? How can I be more efficient and get more done with less?" This is how you should show up each and every day, and leaders aren't exempt—you cannot demand something from someone that you don't do yourself.

- **Leading edge.** In both companies, we strive to think ahead of the *right now* and anticipate our clients' needs before they express them. Our job is to stay ahead of the curve, to stay on top of trends, and to ensure that we're always delivering the most effective products and services to the people we serve. That means research on the marketplace, regular planning meetings with management and advisors, and check-ins with our advisory leadership board.
- **Education and lifelong learning.** We believe it is critical to have intellectual curiosity and to be committed to lifelong learning. No matter how proficient anybody becomes in his or her respective role, there is *always* room to learn and improve. This learning can come from formal education, professional programs, or simply from being open to another way of viewing things. In my firms we encourage and set goals around self-learning through virtual tools and through local class offerings. Employees work with their leaders to set a growth path to achieve short-term and long-term goals. Sometimes learning can come from shadowing another department, or, in my case, another company. It would not be uncommon for someone interested in learning more about financial planning to shadow someone at Private Ocean.

From there, I remind employees at many of the all-hands meetings and company retreats about our values—not by reciting a list but through the telling of a recent experience that illustrates our values in action. You can never reiterate these values often enough to remind your employees of your vision and your goals.

Once you've told them and told them again, though, it's even more important to walk the walk. You can't say one of your core values is being open and honest if you're consistently closing doors, being secretive, and discouraging employees from communicating with you. At Private Ocean, for example, I recently walked by the client services person's desk (the person who greets our clients) and stopped to remind her how lucky our clients are to come in and interact with her! She is always cheerful and helpful as clients come in, and I wanted to make sure she felt appreciated for her contribution to our success. That wasn't paying lip service; everyone in the building recognizes the skills of others and takes the time to express that. You'd be surprised how a little recognition goes a long way in employees' job satisfaction.

Considering Your Audience

You need to approach open and honest communication differently in two situations: large groups (firm-wide) and small groups (or even one-on-one).

My approach is both cases is very similar, in that I am straightforward, casual, and authentic. I have to admit that this is just my style and have found that this communication style resonates with my employees and elicits an honest response. The result is interactions that are refreshingly devoid of political filters that I believe hinder a thriving heart culture.

Large Groups

Talking to larger groups of people is a bit of an art form if you want to make a meaningful, effective impact. It's easy for leaders to go through the motions and remain detached, perhaps even guarded, when addressing a larger group, but that approach does not resonate with people or engage them in caring.

My communication style, both personally and professionally, is to be an open book, generally with a bit of humor thrown in. What you see is what you get, no matter the size or background of the audience. I don't sugarcoat—but I am also not dramatic or prone to stirring up panic.

Speaking to large groups of people can be tricky because your words will be processed and absorbed differently by each individual. What one group may take as good, positive news another may feel is negative and exclusionary. Honest communication builds trust, but the message that goes to a large group needs to be carefully crafted to fit a wide audience with varied concerns and pressure points.

When speaking to large groups, I ask these questions to help steer the right kind of open communication among my teams:

- **How much of this message should I share?** I am always eager to put more out rather than less, as I am not a fan of secrecy for the sake of secrecy. Yes, sometimes there are confidential matters that must be handled carefully and with sensitivity, but I am referring to information that is often kept exclusively to management that could easily be shared—even at a high level—with the rest of the firm. A recent example: Both of my firms are coming up on a lease update for the office. Although many aren't concerned, I wanted to make sure that everyone knew that we were evaluating spaces other than the current office, including the potential locations, considerations and standards, and so on. This approach quickly diminishes any water cooler chatter about hypothetical reasons for, or concerns about, a potential move.

- **Are the other leaders and I in agreement on the message?** The consistency of your management team is key. There is nothing more confusing and unsettling to employees than having one leader telling you one thing and another saying something completely different. You stand to lose credibility fast if your message is not aligned across the team.

- **How will I explain to the group my intention to be open and honest?** I believe the key to opening any conversation is the setup, and delivering an honest and transparent message is no different. In an effort to set context, I'll take a few moments at the beginning of the conversation to clearly explain when information is new, raw, or perhaps changing quickly. I will even point out that I am risking telling them too much too soon because I would rather be open with them—and that I believe they can handle the information. I'll ask them to take the information I am providing as a point in time, let them know that new facts may actually change the message and situation, and really reinforce the unified commitment of the leadership in keeping them up-to-date. How it plays out in reality: "I really feel it's important to share with you X. Some of the information is changing quickly, so please check in with me or your leader to get the most up-to-date information!"

- **Will transparency in this situation be beneficial?**
Remember that line from the movie *A Few Good Men*,
"You can't handle the truth"? I think all leaders have
considered that line when deciding what information
to share with their teams. With transparency comes
change and risk, and for some people the more they
know, the more nerve-racking it is for them to handle
the information. It's like that old adage, "How much
do you want to know about your surgeon?" That he's
an expert with an incredible résumé, or that after hours
he's a raging alcoholic with anger management issues?
That's why you need to decide how much of any giv-
en situation you want to share firm-wide, trusting in
the team you've selected to manage the information
thoughtfully and positively. Transparency is something
I am a huge proponent of, and in my firms it has been
at times the dividing line between the employees who
fit into our culture and those who ultimately do not.
- **Will sharing information help kill speculation?**
Speculation is poison, and unfortunately it is human
nature. We are creative beings, after all, so if you don't
give people the truth, they will fill in a story—and it's
usually not a positive one. They will come to their own
conclusions. They will draft others to support their
ideas and the story will branch off into a million misconceptions. That is why your communications need
not only to be as honest as possible but also carefully
crafted, to fill in any potential holes that may give rise
to questions. For example, I had some news I wanted
to share with the Junxure staff, so I set up a quick all-
hands meeting the following day to discuss it. I'd given

no context for the short, 15-minute meeting; I only wanted to share information via a phone call rather than an email. The subject was innocuous; I simply wanted to tell them personally. During that call I could hear a pin drop in the silent, tense room. I heard later from one of my colleagues that without context, everyone had panicked, and there was lots of speculation on why we were having such a call. It was a lesson learned and reminded me of the precedent I'd set about open and honest communications.

TRANSPARENCY RULES

The saying "Ignorance is bliss" doesn't hold much water in the wealth-management business. We live and breathe in a world in which the more we know, the better we can serve our clients. At Private Ocean last year, the management team was assessing current performance, taking into consideration our business development methods and our advisors as we determined how we could grow. We realized that we had created positions and structures around the advisors that focused more on business development and that didn't adequately serve them, as this particular group—while doing many of the same activities as service advisors—also functioned a bit differently and had activities additional to our other advisors. To help support them and streamline their workflow, the leadership team decided to create a dedicated client services person for the business development group. How we would execute this initiative required some thought and planning, and before we made our first move we brought in our client services people and other advisors for feedback. We wanted to make sure that we gave everyone a heads-up and the opportunity to share their ideas for this new role.

This was an open discussion, and though as a management team we were inclined to move forward, we wanted everyone to know what we were thinking and why. The team agreed it was a good decision to move the initiative forward, and we saw very positive results from the change.

- **Will people feel included?** Regardless of group size, when it comes to being open and honest ask yourself, "How often are my employees surprised by news?" If you find that when you announce something your team is taken off guard, perhaps you haven't been sharing enough information along the way. Surprises are not a good thing in cases in which employees may feel as if they're purposely being excluded from important decisions that affect their lives. That is not to say that employees need to know *everything*—that simply is not possible or productive in some cases. But if you consider how much you *can* share with employees in every situation, your employees will trust your judgment and feel secure in knowing that they'll be kept informed and included in the latest news.

At Private Ocean, for example, we don't waste time when it comes to sharing big news regarding the firm.

If we catch even a hint of the rumor mill starting, or if we've recently been notified of something newsworthy, we immediately have an all-hands meeting or, at the very least, put out a company-wide email with information. Why? Because it's human nature to worry when too many doors are shut for too long.

Recently we experienced issues with our previous office space, which resulted in a lot of confidential, closed-door meetings as we ironed out the details of a move to a more suitable office space. Left without context, people began to interpret this as a sign that something was up—something that was probably not positive. The rumor mill kicked into high gear and questions came up—as did concern.

Without information, people will create a story—and generally not a good one. The imagination tends to run wild, so in this case we quickly pulled everyone together for a meeting. We shared that we were indeed looking to make a positive move to a better location that would address all of our needs and be a wonderful place for clients to visit. We said that we did not have all the answers yet, and the closed doors were simply meant to help us to work out the details before disrupting the office with the news. But going forward, keeping people informed along the way kept rumors to a minimum, as employees believed that as soon as we knew something we would share it with the larger group.

By asking these questions and shaping your message accordingly, what you'll build over time is a reputation for honesty and a proven track record of sharing with staff as much as possible to keep them engaged and informed. Mistakes are inevitable, but people will trust that you have their best interests in mind.

Just remember to be authentic and as complete as you can be with your information. I basically take my conversation with the employees at my firms as far as I can. If I am going to make a mistake it will be from providing *too much* information, and I will stand up for my words.

Small Groups and One-on-One

Speaking to your employees one-on-one or in smaller groups should be a continuation of how you address your employees firm-wide.

As a leader, your employees need to feel as if you hear them, you understand them, and—most of all—that you know and share their goals for personal growth and happiness. Employees should never feel fearful about speaking their minds, and creating an environment that allows for two-way unfiltered conversation must begin with the leader.

How can you achieve that? The key is to provide multiple avenues that foster communication through channels that best suit individual employees. I give my employees several ways to reach me that are based on the methods of communication most comfortable for them.

- **Face-to-face.** Whether it's an impromptu meeting or a planned one-on-one check-in, my door is always open. Beyond that, however, I also make sure to set up social events, such as afternoon picnics and retreats, that create opportunities for casual conversation. I love having these activities, but the planning and execution are absolutely intended to give people a more approachable venue to talk to leaders in the firm, as well as build teams and interact with one another.

- **Phone calls.** Perhaps an employee isn't comfortable knocking on a leader's door or sharing information at a company activity. In that case, employees are welcome to pick up the phone and call me anytime. To facilitate this I always make sure my calendar is up-to-date, so people know when I am available—and they are told that they can *always* call me on my cell phone.

- **Writing versus speaking.** Many leaders have received what I call an email missive. Sometimes they come at midnight and read more like an essay than an email. Technology has given us a variety of ways to express ourselves, and to some this may seem like the safest and most comfortable way to communicate. I see the email missive for what it is—a passionate communication authored by someone who prefers to consider all of his thoughts on a subject before organizing them in a way that best reflects his stance. I take great care in studying these before responding.

- **Using management channels.** Though not my preferred method of communication, some employees feel most comfortable using an intermediary to communicate with leaders. I make no secret about having confidants in both my firms with whom I meet regularly, and who keep me informed on the state/temperature of the firm's culture. These are very positive people in whom employees tend to confide, not because these employees want to keep things confidential, but because they feel more comfortable sharing the buzz with these people than with me. These confidants may be other managers, respected and trusted peers, or one of several so-called culture champions who personify our values. I welcome this approach to communicating because, simply, it works. Just recently a message I wrote was taken out of context and affected some employees negatively. One of my confidants was quickly notified and I made a point to reach out to those employees immediately, to clear the air. Never wait to fix a supposedly small problem; it's these seemingly insignificant miscommunications that often lead to larger gaps in perception down the road.

If, like me, you have a firm that is geographically spread out and not set up for in-person meetings, I recommend making technology work in your favor to bridge the distance. Beyond the usual technological means of communication, you might implement an instant message system that allows employees to "talk" in real time. Consider using an Intranet or internal wiki to ensure that employees have constant exposure to department projects and development plans. Also, I highly recommend taking advantage of video conferencing applications, such as Skype, Adobe Connect, GoToMeeting, or even FaceTime (for iPhone or iPad users), to have face-to-face conversations with employees one-on-one.

Being accessible to all of your employees is definitely not an easy task, but as a leader it's your responsibility to make yourself available. That doesn't mean people will be able to find you 24/7, but you do need to set aside time for people to talk to you. And unless you're a company with 25,000 employees, I don't think it's unreasonable to dedicate a few minutes of your week to this purpose. In my firms everyone has direct access to me, and that directly correlates to our values.

The 55–38–7 Communication Formula

Why am I such a huge advocate for in-person (or at the very least, in-video) conferencing communications? According to researcher Albert Mehrabian's findings from two communication studies (Mehrabian and Wiener in 1967[2] and Mehrabian and Ferris, also in 1967[3]), 55 percent of communication is visual (nonverbal) and takes the form of body language and eye contact, 38 percent is vocal (the pitch, speed, tone, and volume of speech), and 7 percent involves actual words. Given these statistics, it makes sense for a leader to devote face-to-face time to employees, not only to hear what they have to say but also to actually see what they're really feeling and thinking.

The Mehrabian Communication Model

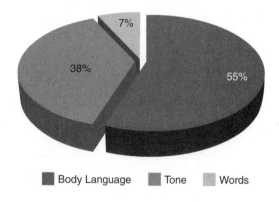

■ Body Language   ■ Tone   ■ Words

Even though video conferencing helps immensely when you cannot meet in person, I still cannot stress enough how crucial a leader's physical presence is to creating and cultivating heart culture. In all fairness to employees, the reality is that in order to encourage honest communication, you (as the leader) will need to prod sometimes. You will need to ask questions. At Private Ocean I periodically meet with each advisor and with each team. And at Junxure I make a point to travel to its office once every few months to stay connected. We also plan annual retreats for both companies that from a professional standpoint are conducive to development and project planning. From a personal perspective, these retreats also remind employees that they're just as engaged with the business and responsible for preserving the firm's unique culture as the leadership team is. Investing in a two-day event each year pays dividends in buoying attitudes and inspiring motivation to continue on the path of success as a team.

Creating a culture that encourages honest communication between an employee and a leader can be a huge challenge, and that is why it's important to create multiple ways to tackle the concepts. In the end, what you want to get across to your employees is simply that their voices are heard.

I have been accused of wearing my heart on my sleeve, and I will admit that sometimes I do. I truly care about my employees, and when you're emotionally invested in your business and your people, that genuine emotion will be apparent. This is not a bad thing.

I should stop for a moment and say that I have a very direct, very open communication style that does not vary, no matter whom I am speaking to. My approach is to start by asking questions and listen to the answers. I share my point of view, but internally I am always assessing where the person is coming from and what his or her motives are.

Even when an employee manages to ruffle my feathers (you cannot have heart culture without real emotion), I make sure to convey to that person that he is free to speak, and that this is a safe space where what is said will have no consequences or negative impacts on his job or reputation—as long as he is respectful and constructive.

What Is the Safe Space?

A former colleague of mine, whom I hold in very high regard, came into my office many years ago and asked to speak freely to me. At the time I thought I was a good leader and a good communicator, and I did not know what he might want to address with me.

This colleague was concerned that I might take his comments personally, so he asked for a "safe space." I complied.

What happened next took the wind out of me. I received feedback about my leadership style that really hurt. He was very professional, but his comments hit home. He had preconceived notions about me that I was unaware of, and he was clearly unhappy with me as a leader.

That interaction with my colleague was one of the very first times where I sat quietly and assessed what was being communicated. I was careful not to shut him down or to discourage him from continuing. But inside I was angry! I was absolutely livid! I wanted to defend my position and explain that his misconceptions were just that. But instead I sat quietly, and when he was finished I responded by saying, "Okay, you've brought up some really good points, and let me think about what you've said and get back to you." That was 180 degrees opposite from my natural makeup.

You see, I come from a very verbal family accustomed to sparring with one another, in which I am the youngest. The goal back then was to be heard among a chorus of strong, opinionated voices, but that approach does not serve you or anyone very well in the business world. When a decision must be strategic, collaborative, and well planned, the last thing you want to do is react before thinking—or worse, unintentionally attack someone's views because they conflict with your own. In the past if such a situation arose, my instinct would be to react and push forth my ideas. Now I appreciate the wisdom of silence. I try not to be reactionary; I listen and assess the situation before I share my ideas about what I feel would be the most beneficial steps to a solution.

If you're faced with a situation in which a colleague or employee may be holding back from having a difficult conversation, or if she seems to have trepidation about approaching you with a concern or issue, offer up the safe place. Say to her, "Everything you say for the next few minutes is safe and confidential. Whatever the issue is, we will figure it out." What you'll find is that a few words of acknowledgment and comfort will help build enough trust to open the lines of communication.

Just remember to think before you respond and to be ready for the honesty that you have just encouraged.

Resolving Conflict

In any firm, there will inevitably be occasions when you are confronting challenges, issues, ideas, or strategies and not everyone is in agreement on how to proceed. (If everyone always agrees with you, you have a bigger problem.) Disagreements are healthy and should be expected, but how you resolve these differences will determine how your employees feel, not only about the situation itself but also about your company's culture. At Private Ocean, one thing we (the leadership team) do really well is communicate our rules of engagement. In the event of a conflict or difference of opinion, the first thing we do is slow things down.

This may seem counterintuitive, but often when ideas are being tossed out and emotions are running high, the best thing you can do is slow things down. We make sure every voice is heard unimpeded. Everyone is careful and respectful with their language, focusing only on the issue and their perspectives. We have cultivated an environment in which everybody is very willing to see other points of view and recognize that people are coming from different places on a subject. We take the time and work hard to arrive at a place everyone can live with. So though we may disagree and get passionate, we are all willing to ultimately compromise for the good of the firm and our clients. No one walks out the door without feeling as if he's been heard and that he's played a role in the final decision. Finally, everyone agrees to support the decision—no undermining things or talking negatively about it.

Walking the Walk

Honest communication is only half the equation. Convincing others that you are a person of your word requires building trust, and that does not happen overnight. This trust comes from setting an example of transparency and consistency through your actions.

For example, delivering extreme service is something we consider very important to our business. At both Private Ocean and Junxure, our entire value system is based on the client being king. The Private Ocean client deserves fast, excellent advice and service. Junxure customers deserve +1 service, so they deserve the best technology available from the most qualified individuals. That's why we strive to always think beyond the now, and we encourage our employees to do the same. Everyone's ideas are welcome and all are expected to have this +1 mind-set, from the person who answers the first phone call to the principal of the firm. There are no excuses and no one is exempt.

As a leader, never think for a second that your employees don't look to you to set the example for what you lay out as the firm's fundamental values. Should emails and phone calls be answered in a timely manner? Then you, too, must maintain that standard. Should leaders meet with their employees in regular one-on-ones? Then you, too, should make time to meet with your direct reports.

At this point, you may be asking yourself, "Who has time for all that? Is that not why you delegate?"

Nobody said being an effective leader is easy. I have heard the saying "The fish rots from the head down," and it's true. If someone on the front lines is treating your clients poorly, it's likely that someone is treating her poorly. Just remember, culture begins and ends in the same place: at the top.

If you're feeling as if dedicating so much time to nurturing morale and maintaining a healthy culture might be not only overwhelming but impossible, consider this: Studies have shown that higher morale equals higher profitability.

Honesty and Integrity Recap: Tips to Remember

- Your communication should always reinforce your beliefs, therefore setting a standard for employees to use as a guide when interacting with their leaders, their coworkers, and even your clients.
- As a leader, never think for a second that your employees don't look to you to set the example for what you lay out as the firm's fundamental values.
- Provide multiple avenues that foster communication through channels that best suit individual employees. People have different ways to communicate, so give them several ways to reach you. In the end, what you want to get across to your employees is simply that their voices are heard.
- *Walk your talk!* Your actions *do* speak louder than your words!

Benefits

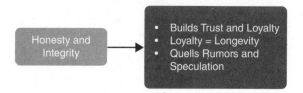

Notes

1. Patrick Lencioni, *Getting Naked: A Business Fable about Shedding the Three Fears That Sabotage Client Loyalty* (San Francisco: Jossey-Bass, 2010).
2. Albert Mehrabian and Morton Wiener, "Decoding of Inconsistent Communications," *Journal of Personality and Social Psychology* 6, no. 1 (1967): 109–114, doi:10.1037/h0024532. PMID 6032751.
3. Albert Mehrabian and Susan R. Ferris, "Inference of Attitudes from Nonverbal Communication in Two Channels," *Journal of Consulting Psychology* 31, no. 3 (1967): 248–252, doi:10.1037/h0024648.

Chapter 3

Compassion

Unlocking the Secret to a People-First Culture

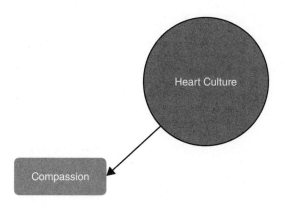

S ome firms have figured out that the secret to a successful culture is to put people first. What does that mean, exactly?

It means that a firm is intentional about considering the individual needs of its employees because it wants a workforce of happy, passionate, loyal people who feel valued, respected, and heard.

Now, I don't think any business owner intentionally disregards company culture, but the biggest issue I have seen is that some leaders don't know much about the people who work for them. Some of the biggest missteps—failing to develop potential employees and not rewarding and recognizing achievements—are the result of being unaware or from miscommunications that can easily be remedied.

Ask yourself how well you know your employees. I know as firms grow it gets more and more difficult to remember spouses' and children's names and personal interests. But just like it's a leader's job to know an employee's personal work goals, it's just as important to know their personal life goals and what motivates them both at work and at home.

If that seems like a tall order, you are right! That's why I am an advocate for using technology to help you keep your mind organized.

For example, financial advisors rely on their client relationship management (CRM) system to keep track of all of the details pertaining to their clients. Why not use your CRM for your employees as well?

I think of my staff as my most valuable clients. After all, these are the people with whom I work side-by-side, who help me to reach my own goals, and who help take care of our clients. I don't have to remind myself that I only get as far as we as a company get together.

Besides the usual methods of showing appreciation, including compensation, time off, bonuses, and the like, there is a lot to be said about individual recognition for performance, contribution, dedication, and for the simple fact that you enjoy working with the person—just checking in.

Technology makes it possible to remember birthdays, for instance, and I have calendar reminders set up for everyone's birthday and work anniversaries. I make a point, either in person or by phone, to check in with all employees twice a year on these special days to ask how they are doing and how their families are, and to remind them how much they are appreciated and recognized for who they are and the work they bring to the business. It's a small thing, yes, but it's the small things that add up to big things.

Okay, at the moment that amounts to 150 calls for me that each last about 15 minutes (or 37.5 hours a year). Am I busy? Yes. Am I late calling some days because I am traveling or I am holed up in back-to-back meetings? Yes. But I always make the time available for every employee, and I always make those calls. They are worth every second of my time, and now, so many years after this tradition began, the birthday and anniversary calls have become an institution.

I recently made a birthday call to an employee who had only been with the firm for a few months. I began the call with, "Do you know why I am calling?" and his response— "Are you kidding? I have been waiting for this call!"— spoke volumes to me. Apparently his colleagues had clued him in on my tradition, and he was looking forward to the call.

A little recognition goes a long way, and all it costs you is maybe 5 to 15 minutes of your time. There is no agenda on these calls, no task being assigned, and no ulterior motive. I am told that for employees, it's refreshing. They feel appreciated. They feel recognized as people, not as numbers or titles, and it reinforces the values you set for your firm.

Putting people first means creating a corporate culture with its own unique soul. That soul is at the core of your business and at the foundation of your company's DNA. The people who exist in this culture are a part not only of nurturing that soul but also protecting it.

Recently one of my firms lost one of its truly key players to a large company known for its stellar work environment and culture, and very high salaries. This person's departure was a real loss for us, and as we take such care to hire the right person for a specific role, she was not easily replaced.

Months went by and we faced real challenges finding someone who could not only take on the role but who could also fit into our team during a very busy time. Eventually my leadership team and I discussed what action we should take, and we all agreed that we needed to reach out to her and ask if she'd consider returning.

Though we had little hope that she would accept our offer, I called her personally and let her know four things:

1. She made a difference and would have a great impact on the company.
2. She was one of a kind—and important to us!
3. She was needed to help us succeed.
4. She was part of our family.

She ended up taking our offer and returning to the firm. When I spoke to her, she said some very interesting things that reinforced for me the power of our culture. She said, "This place is like coming home. Everyone here has a voice. Everyone matters. It's like being in a family where no one is trying to outdo anyone—in fact, we're all here because we passionately believe in doing the right thing for our customers."

That, she said, mattered more to her than bright, shiny perks and a giant salary. She wanted to make a difference. This was her contribution.

It's surprising to me that many companies still don't employ a people-first culture; one that's based on compassion and heart. Here are some of the overall trends we've noted over the years:

- **Increased engagement and enthusiasm from employees who feel invested in the company.** We work hard as a team, so it makes sense that everyone in the firm should enjoy the rewards of success. When the leaders at Private Ocean set a goal of hitting a billion dollars in assets under management, the team was supportive and enthusiastic. To celebrate hitting that milestone we planned to treat the entire firm to an offsite trip to an Arizona resort. Pictures of the resort were shown each month as results were tracked and reported.

- **Higher performance levels.** Happy employees are present employees. At both my firms incentives for individual and company performance led to higher productivity within the office and increased profitability.

- **Strong employee loyalty that leads to higher retention rates.** The average tenure of an employee at Private Ocean is over six years. In both companies our turnover rate is very low, and some former employees even return.
- **Less conflict between employees and management when focus is placed on a shared goal.** Everyone shares the same goal of delighting the client, so people take extraordinary measures to deliver on their commitments. In the event they are unable to take care of the client, someone is always willing to step up, without question, to help them complete their tasks.
- **Higher morale stemming from individual recognition and inclusion.** A team mentality is a key component of the culture at Private Ocean. An employee recently drafted a lighthearted theme song for the firm, which mentioned nearly everyone by name and went over so well that the team often gathers to perform the chorus live.

Morale and Profitability

As if the benefits listed previously weren't enough to motivate you to consider a people-first culture, several studies have shown that companies with higher morale are also more profitable.

Research gathered by David Sirota and Douglas A. Klein for the book *The Enthusiastic Employee* showed that in 2012 high-morale companies outperformed their industry competitors by 368 percent in terms of year-over-year stock market returns.[1]

And in a study of high performance work practices of nearly 1,000 firms representing all major industries, Jeffrey Pfeffer and John F. Veiga wrote, "A one standard deviation improvement in the human resources system created a 7.05 percent decrease in turnover and, on a per employee basis, $27,044 more in sales and $18,641 and $3,814 more in market value and profits, respectively."[2]

A poor culture with low morale can be costly for a business over time, with higher turnover rates, employee dissatisfaction, and absenteeism all playing a role. In a study done by Wolters Kluwer, CCH, on unscheduled absences in 2007, some of the largest employers in the United States estimated that unscheduled absences cost their businesses more than $760,000 per year in direct payroll costs.[3] Just as surprising, the study also found that two-thirds of workers in the United States who call in sick at the last minute aren't actually ill. While personal illness accounts for 34 percent of unscheduled absences, 66 percent of absences are due to stress, personal issues, an attitude of entitlement, or family issues. And since the vast majority of our industry consists of small businesses, remember—if you are a company of five people and one is out, that is 20 percent of your workforce!

Differentiating "Me" Culture from Heart Culture

In one of my previous jobs, I worked in an environment that was not only competitive but also incredibly self-centered. Leaders took all credit for any of the ideas or

work an employee put forward, and they pitted employees against one another for recognition and rewards, such
that even someone showing great improvement and development was often overshadowed by a star performer and
overlooked. I think that's incredibly detrimental to a company. I call this *"me" culture*—as in, "How is this about me?"
or "What's in this for me?"

A byproduct of me culture is that the focus on competing and beating out coworkers can easily extend to
the relationship between leaders and employees. In such
a scenario it may not necessarily be in the leader's interest
for an employee to succeed. If employees outperform or
outshine a leader, for example, they may be construed as
threats. The leader may then undermine—consciously or
unconsciously—an employee's work and reputation.

When a leader is not focused on people and their success first, problems arise that are difficult to overcome once
this kind of foundation is established (I don't trust you, you
don't care about me, you're out to get me, etc.). Trust and
confidence are easy to lose and incredibly hard to reestablish once these feelings are present.

I recognize that in any given workplace there are issues
with people having to do with competition and compatibility. Sometimes personalities clash and that is unavoidable.
However, leaders can overcome these conflicts (or lessen
their impact) by laying a foundation of open communication that is based on mutual respect and a shared focus on
the same goal—in our industry, that's figuring out how to
best serve our clients. There needs to be a structure for mutual success: One person's success should not limit another
person's opportunities.

John: The Self-Centered (and Insecure) Leader

As a young man about to graduate from high school, I worked as a part-time forklift operator for a retail warehouse chain. The warehouse manager, with whom I had almost no interaction, seemed to not like me personally. I could speculate about why John (not his real name) didn't like me, but speculation is not helpful. However, I can say that his dislike for me had nothing to do with performance, or attendance, or attitude.

With graduation fast approaching, my father surprised me with a trip to Hawaii as my graduation present. Excited, I asked John for a week off (this was months in advance) and informed him that I had even secured someone to take my place. John denied my request outright yet did not give me a reason. I tried to talk with him, even emphasizing that I had made arrangements with a friend to cover my shifts according to company guidelines, but he just refused to grant the time off.

Now, retail is a tough business. There are many situations in which you're encouraged not to communicate and not to raise your hand with new ideas. The general mentality in these environments is to not rock the boat, but I didn't believe in that back then and I certainly don't endorse that culture now. I am outspoken and I like to share ideas, and I encourage my employees to do the same. In this particular situation, my boss seemed unreasonable and unable to communicate on any level. It felt as if he just wanted to exert his dominance and control over me.

Worse, John seemed unhappy in general, and much of his unhappiness was focused on me personally. My smallest success made him more antagonistic toward me, and denying my request gave him the power he needed to reassert his superiority over me. What wasn't considered was the impact this one act—and one very bad example of leadership—had not only on me but on my coworkers and others in the company. To say the least, it was not motivating to others!

Ironically, when I told my father I couldn't go he called the company CEO, who was a personal friend, and asked if there was something that could be done—and of course the warehouse manager was instructed to let me go. I didn't know anything about this, but a few days after my vacation request was denied he called me in and angrily told me that he "didn't know who I knew, but my vacation request was approved." And he was angry! John came across as insecure and petty to me, and his actions seemed driven by personal issues. His unreasonable treatment of me seemed personal, and all of my coworkers watched this—and it did not inspire anyone!

I worked for him for another six months until he got transferred to another warehouse. From there he disappeared off the company's grid.

CHANGING COURSE: GOING FROM "ME" TO "WE"

What happens when you realize that you've fostered a dog-eat-dog culture in which your employees feel as if they have to compete against one another to succeed?

It's a tough reality, but if you're surrounded by "me" people you probably have "me" leaders. Changing this will take lots of work and you have to begin by looking inward at yourself as a leader. What have you done or not done to create a healthy company culture? What steps can you take to change course? Second, you need to take a hard look at your employees and ask yourself who has the potential to help steer the ship back on course and who is contributing to the negativity. Change is difficult to come by, takes time and patience, and is—in some cases—impossible without staff changes. You're probably going to have to make some key people decisions and find leaders who can help reground your firm and promote positive change and adoption of it.

In wealth management, as in many other industries, there will be advisors or business development people with competitive goals that may—unwittingly or not—pit one employee against another. At Private Ocean each advisor has a goal, but it is customized for that one person. We consider the workload, capacity, client load, and business development skills of each person to create a goal that works for that employee and incentivizes him to perform. We also have a compensation structure that rewards collaboration in getting new clients.

So instead of employees being against *one another*, this structure means an employee is basically *for* herself—and the company—and it is all about her own personal and professional development. If an advisor doesn't hit a personal goal no one benefits or bests that person. An employee has goals that align with the firm's goals and everyone is working toward the same target. Yes, there is a bit of peer pressure, but it's more in line with wanting to show up for the team. People have expectations of one another no matter the role, and they rely on one another to perform because success only comes as a team.

Another key element is that we try to foster an environment where one person's opportunity doesn't come at the expense of another's. If an opportunity comes along, say a new position or promotion, the team knows that the candidate chosen will be best suited for that particular role. So while a client services person may not get a certain kind of manager's role, it doesn't mean he can't pursue another opportunity within the firm—for example, a certificate to become a paraplanner or a position in investment operations. We are constantly looking to help others grow, and we communicate often that we prefer to promote from within and train the right people. Keeping that door open for future opportunities empowers employees to consider the possibilities.

With heart culture, every interaction between a leader and an employee is based on mutual respect and a genuine focus on what's best for everyone involved. It's the slow building of a relationship, one that begins with the very first recruiting phone call, continues through ongoing one-on-one meetings, and grows over time. That relationship even extends to when employees find their paths are leading them somewhere else.

Take a recent situation in the software company, in which one of our top performers resigned to take a high-level position at another firm. This was a player in a key position during a time that the company truly depended on him. It was heartbreaking to lose him, and inside I was personally hurt when I first got the news. Not that this is a bad thing, mind you, as it means you care about the people you work with. But if a leader is truly focused on people first, then the last thing he or she should do is stand in the way of someone's dreams and opportunities. I had several conversations with the employee, who graciously gave a month's notice and reached out to me personally to tell me he was leaving and to help with the transition. I knew that this new role was something he was passionate about and that the role was a great opportunity in which he wouldn't be competing with us, and I was happy for him. The best thing I could do as a leader in this situation was to acknowledge his value and contribution to the firm and to wish him well—and even help him on his journey. In return, the employee said to me that my reaction to his news—and the support I gave him—made his decision even harder than he'd imagined.

A side note to this—it is not a coincidence that numerous employees in my firms have left to go on to other firms, only to return because they could not replace the unique, caring, family atmosphere that we've cultivated. To me, that says a lot about the lasting impact the right culture has on its employees.

Compassion Recap: Tips to Remember

- Ask yourself how well you know your employees. Even a little recognition and personal acknowledgment goes a long way, so take advantage of everything available to you—leaders, technology, and personal check-ins—to stay connected to everyone on your team.
- Assess your current culture—do people work well together, or do they have a "me" attitude? If it's the latter, start thinking about the cause of this mentality and what you can do to start encouraging collaboration to build a sense of team.
- Set reminders if necessary to acknowledge employees periodically and consistently in a positive way. It is far too easy to overlook good work and call out employees' mistakes.

Benefits

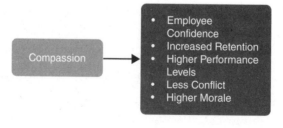

Notes

1. David Sirota and Douglas A. Klein, *The Enthusiastic Employee: How Companies Profit by Giving Workers What They Want*, 2nd ed. (Upper Saddle River, NJ: Pearson Education, 2013).
2. Jeffrey Pfeffer and John F. Veiga, "Putting People First for Organizational Success," *Academy of Management Executive* 13, no. 2 (1999): 37–48.
3. Wolters Kluwer, CCH, *Unscheduled Absence Survey* (Riverwoods, IL: Wolters Kluwer, CCH, 2007).

Chapter 4

Respect

Promoting Personal Growth, the Key to Inspiring Motivation

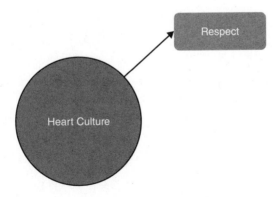

H ave you ever worked for a company that took your professional goals into account when planning for the future of your role? In my experience, when employees are given the flexibility to explore something they're passionate about, they'll work twice as hard to achieve their goals. Does that mean a compromise for the business? Possibly. But as I described in Chapter 1, hiring people with the same philosophy and goals that govern your firm can help you reach goals that may previously have been unattainable. In my case I wanted to be a financial advisor because I wanted to help people, and the toolkit I wanted to use was financial planning. When I hire, I am looking for people with that same goal—*to help people*.

One thing that really gets to me is that I cannot give 100 percent all the time to either of my companies, and that's why I am very choosy about my leadership team. I need to be able to lean on leaders who can be as encouraging and focused on the personal growth of people as I am. Why? Because promoting personal goals and supporting employees' passion to grow in something they love is the key to inspiring motivation.

What it all comes down to, simply, is respect. Respect for others and their goals, respect for their happiness, and a mutual respect for the business.

HAPPY EMPLOYEES, HEALTHY PROFITS

In her book *Make More Money by Making Your Employees Happy*, Dr. Noelle C. Nelson references a study from the Jackson Organization that showed that "companies that effectively appreciate employee value enjoy a return on equity and assets more than triple that experienced by firms that don't. When looking at *Fortune*'s '100 Best Companies to Work For' stock prices rose an average of 14 percent per year from 1998 to 2005, compared to 6 percent for the overall market."

Michael: The Demotivational Leader

Right out of graduate school, I got a job at a company as a financial advisor working for a sales manager. This manager was your old-school sales manager who basically treated all employees the same—no matter what you did, it wasn't enough.

To put this in context, our office was one of the highest ranked locations of this firm nationally, and I was one of the top performers (among new employees) in the office.

Michael (not his real name) had one playbook for motivation, and it had nothing to do with personal growth. He had a "What have you done for me lately" attitude, and the culture within the department was one in which no matter what you accomplished or how good your results were, you were lectured on how you should have done more.

What I learned quickly was that for each success or accolade, employees were quickly—and I mean within a day—fielding questions such as, "Why didn't you do *this*?" and "If you could do this, why didn't you do that?" And, "How much more will you do next month?"

So no matter how well I performed, what I accomplished, or how good my results were, his praise quickly became a lesson in what I needed to do next time. It was annoying to me, and to many of my colleagues it was demeaning.

My last interaction with Michael was a goal-setting meeting, and having exceeded my previous goals considerably, I was already confident about what I could accomplish. We were sitting on the thirty-third floor of a high-rise in downtown San Francisco, overlooking the bay.

He proceeded to deliver another of his lectures on how I needed to hit higher goals. When he was finished, I calmly said to him that I was an incredibly motivated person, and that I had personal goals that far exceeded anything he could ever set for me. I told him that I found these conversations to be the most demotivating approach I'd ever encountered, and that the day I needed *him* to set my goals was the day that I would jump out of that thirty-third-floor window.

As you can imagine he was furious, and by then I was fully prepared to quit. I spoke with the regional vice president, who of course was told about my comments, and he pulled me aside to apologize, recognizing what had happened and that one leader had negatively affected a good performer. From then on the reporting structure changed, and I was given more autonomy to work on my own without a micromanager.

Motivation is an interesting concept. It has been said that you as a leader cannot motivate people—but you can certainly *demotivate* people. To a large extent I believe that is true, and I feel that my role as a leader is to inspire and support people to do their best work and to do everything I can to make that happen.

HOW TO LOSE EMPLOYEES AND DEMOTIVATE PEOPLE

David Mamet may have illustrated it best in *Glengarry Glen Ross*, his 1984 play that won a Pulitzer Prize and a Tony, when the motivational trainer says to a group of real estate agents, "As you all know, first prize is a Cadillac El Dorado. Anyone want to see second prize? Second prize is a set of steak knives. Third prize is you're fired."

Though this particular scenario seems incredibly harsh, many of us have been in similar situations, in which the motivation to perform was based on fear. Nothing sends good, talented employees to online job search sites faster than a leader who doesn't value people first.

Motivation comes from different places for different people. Personally, I am a motivated person from my core. I work with people who are also motivated and that plays very heavily into the hiring process.

Now, as a good leader you can inspire people through supportive, caring, positive leadership. You can encourage people to feel as if they're part of your team by being straight, open, and honest about your business and where it's going; by treating them fairly; and by expressing your appreciation.

Helping Employees Explore What Motivates Them

When I or my management team has conversations with employees, we regularly check in with their goals and gauge how their current position is aligned with their needs. We ask questions like, "What is it you want to do in your career? Where do you want to go in life? What do you feel most passionate about in your work?"

I always want to recognize and acknowledge a person's strengths, and encourage him or her to develop and use those strengths. In the case of one particular employee, for example, I was impressed with his ability to write in a way that resonated with our clients. So he ended up writing our client letters and our website content. There's no rule that says a certain type of employee is only allowed to do one job. That would be like assuming that people only like one flavor of ice cream or one sport.

Taking into consideration the needs of the firm, what I do is talk to people about what interests them and then assess their current skill sets. Then I work with management to see how we can match what we need with the path people envision for themselves. I am not the type of leader who is fixated on tight job descriptions that are superimposed on the firm. I am willing to be flexible with people and try to help them along in the direction that they want to go in their careers. The impact of this realization on an employee is considerable and immediate any time I have these conversations, and in many cases, what the company ends up with is a highly motivated person willing to prove himself to achieve his goals.

Also, by offering these opportunities, the employee does not feel competitive and does not feel stifled by her current position. The idea of potential growth is enough to motivate her to carve out her own path.

Here are some great real-life examples of this approach from my businesses.

- **Building trust and growing pains.** At Private Ocean, many of my staff have been with me for years, growing from one role into the next. Years ago I hired someone as a key client services person who was an incredible go-getter; from her first days she was always looking for ways to improve process and to make a difference. At the time I needed additional help and she stepped up into a position that wasn't easy. I was zero for two with executive assistants, and delegation was getting tougher for me. In this position there needed to be an ample amount of communication and trust built up over time, so that meant starting with small projects together to build rapport. As our confidence in each other grew, I asked this person to help me with both of my businesses as I recognized her ability to observe people and situations in ways that I had missed. She is an invaluable asset and continues to grow, has taken on the role of managing institutional relationships for the software company, and is also involved in leadership and high-level strategic discussions.

- **A new department.** Years ago we had evolved to a point where it was time to assess and expand our product-testing processes at Junxure. That led to a decision to create a separate internal quality assurance (QA) department. We looked at either hiring the best qualified candidates to spearhead this new department or building from within the company and creating new opportunities for talented existing employees. In our culture we want to promote from within. This was the perfect opportunity to have discussions with people who had the most experience using our programs—if not the exact qualifications of a QA specialist.

So I worked with our management team to approach several senior members of our technical support team to gauge their interest in taking on a new role. Before explaining the company's need we asked, "How do you see yourself growing within the company? Are you looking into continuing in the technical field or do your interests lie elsewhere? Are you hoping to grow into a supervisory role?" These discussions were incredibly helpful for the company to gauge interest and motivation, but they also reminded the employees that their leaders not only were paying attention to their needs and goals, they also were helping them create individual security. There's nothing more powerful than feeling as if you've got some control over your personal destiny.

Once we finished these discussions the management team determined that we had incredible internal resources that should be given the opportunity to take on the roles in our newly formed QA department. Was it an investment of our time? Yes. We could have hired an outside resource easily. But this is our culture, and this one act strengthened a bond with key players and inspired others to believe that their own personal goals could be achieved. What we ended up with was a fiercely loyal and dedicated QA team who felt a strong sense of accomplishment. And, as a leader, all I needed to do was ask the question, "What do you need from me to be successful?"

- **Boomerangs.** In both my firms, we have a handful of so-called boomerang employees—incredibly talented and motivated people who fit perfectly with our culture, but whose situations took them away from the company. For these employees the door is never quite shut, and when possible we welcome them back in new roles.

- **Amicable separation.** Employee separations are never easy, but as a leader in a heart culture you must ultimately have the confidence and the right philosophical outlook to admit when an employee's personal goals don't align with the company's. Years ago one of my most trusted colleagues decided that he wanted to branch out on his own. He was (and is) immensely talented and intelligent, and is definitely a team player with heart, so I expressed my support and offered to connect him with people I thought could offer him advice on his new role. I also reminded him that the door was always open. Years later this colleague became a business partner and now we frequently refer business to each other's firms. Our mutually amicable separation has been profitable for both companies and has proven that with mutual trust and respect relationships may change but don't necessarily have to end. We are great friends and continue to work together—albeit in different companies.

Obviously, there will be cases (unlike the last example) when what employees really want to do is far out of scope from what the company needs or what employees have the skill set to achieve. In these cases I encourage them to explore their options for school, training, and even outside opportunities. Always be fair and empathetic to what a person needs, recognizing that a happy future for that individual is likely not going to be at your company. However, while he's at the company, it's important that he stays focused and engaged with what he is there to accomplish. In my experience it has been tremendously beneficial to *not* burn bridges.

THE CASE FOR HUMAN RESOURCES

It's an individual choice for firms to determine how involved the human resources department is in a company's culture. In my firm, the human resource function primarily centers on keeping employees informed about benefits and policies and acting as a sounding board for both leaders and employees looking for guidance in those areas. And there is certainly an important role for human resources when someone is significantly underperforming or not responding to feedback.

Consider human resources as another line of defense in protecting your culture. Brainstorm with the human resources team when an employee may be the right person for the firm but not quite right in his current role. What skills does this person have that got him hired in the first place? How could the employee and the company benefit from finding a more suitable role for him?

An example of this is when we placed someone in a team lead position but found he wasn't comfortable in that role. At the same time we had another challenge we were wrestling with, and when we sat down to talk to this employee about his challenges, we asked for his help on this other issue. He offered an idea to restructure the team that would put him in this other role that suited his skill set perfectly. This made him happy, helped the firm, and everyone won. The key to that resolution was maintaining mutual respect.

Keeping Tabs

Our approach to staying aligned with employee goals is to foster open communication. Even the annual review is more of a conversation that is as much self-assessment and company assessment as it is leadership assessing the employee. We send out a questionnaire to employees at year-end that is centered on how employees feel about their roles and their accomplishments, and how the company is supporting them in their endeavors. This feedback loop is key to helping us gauge the current cultural climate, what the *firm* is doing well (and not doing well), and the alignment of employees' opinion of their performance with a leader's.

The annual review, however, is really a formality when you make regular check-ins with employees. Each one of those should be intentional and purposeful, no matter how casual the conversation. One of the things I ask any employee I happen to be speaking to is, "How are things going? Are you getting what you need?" Asking two very simple questions may take employees off guard the first time you ask, but by the second or third time you'll be surprised by people's honesty. Then there are the extended conversations over lunch or at a company outing in which I pose questions like, "How do you feel about your personal development? Where do you want to take your career? How can I help you accomplish your goals?" These kinds of questions really play off the skills used by advisors, since our job is to ask clients these very same questions and truly care about the answers. What I try not to do is to put artificial limits on people. I look at people and try to see what they are capable of and how to help them see what they're capable of, and encourage them to do it.

Cultivating relationships focused on an individual employee's goals is an immeasurably successful factor in my firms' employee retention rates. There is a sense of pride in my firms in how many years someone has been with the company. It gives employees a familial feeling of belonging to something special, as well as a sense of professional accomplishment with their personal growth.

Here are some tips that I recommend to help inspire your employees by encouraging personal growth:

- **Stop trying to fit everyone in a box.** You don't have to forget that a planner, a client services associate, or an IT professional has certain job priorities and responsibilities. What you should think about, how-ever, is making sure that your employees feel confi-dent about expressing other interests that may enhance their work experiences. As a leader it's also your job to ask questions and explore the direction in which your employees are headed. Nurture their strengths while also developing their opportunities to improve weaker areas. You never know where a good idea is going to come from.

- **Lead, don't manage.** You invested a lot of time into making sure that you hired the right person for the job, so it's time you trusted her to take the reins. Empower-ing people to make decisions, supporting them, guiding them, and then getting out of the way helps promote a sense of ownership in the business.

- **Map out a mutually beneficial plan.** Listen to what your employees want for their futures. Start with the right now, then ask them to look out three, five, and ten years. Help map out a plan that's benefi-cial for the employee as well as for your firm. Do you have a client services employee interested in invest-ments? Have you considered expanding your invest-ment committee? Help your firm grow right along with your people.

- **Be ready to adjust that plan.** Things change, and that's okay. Say someone wants to go back to school to get an advanced degree. Does it benefit your firm? Does this person show potential as being a part of your succession plan? Do your best to adapt to the changing tides.

Last, when it comes to encouraging personal growth, instead of keeping score and focusing on just wins and losses, strive for a culture that expects constant change and promotes ongoing improvements that can lead to bigger success over time. This helps strengthen the team mentality and encourages employees to think both as individuals and as vital members of the team. The goal is to always be asking, "How can I do this better next time?" and more important, "How can *we* do this better next time?"

One more thing—it is vital when trying things that don't work out as expected that there not be a *cost* to the person who tried it or suggested it. Employees need to feel safe innovating; otherwise they won't take risks in trying things that can make huge differences in efficiency and client service.

Respect Recap: Tips to Remember

- Ask your employees for honest feedback on where they envision themselves in five years. If it makes sense to the business, it may be beneficial to both parties to expand on roles that give employees a sense of growth and accomplishment.
- Be flexible in your job descriptions and roles going forward.
- Empowering people to make decisions, supporting them, guiding them, and then getting out of the way helps promote a sense of ownership in the business. That is being a good leader.

Benefits

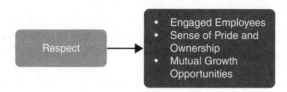

Chapter 5

Persistence and Consistency

Maintaining Employee Relationships

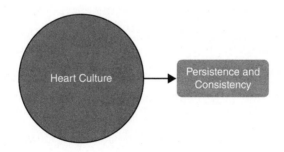

O ne of the most challenging aspects of heart-based
leadership is maintaining a healthy, caring culture once you've hired the right people, set clear

goals, and communicated your values and philosophy. Why? Well, as a leader you're expected to keep the entire body in motion: looking out for the company's overall financial well-being as well as planning for growth, obstacles, and surprises. Leaders need to be aware that a culture is constantly evolving to meet the needs of its employees. To adapt you should regularly assess and communicate what matters most to both the employee and the firm. Finding the balance between your core values and the evolving needs of your employees will help with employee retention down the road.

No issue in a firm is so small or insignificant that you don't have a vested interest in its outcome. And as advisors, many of you can also relate to what I call *entrepreneurial paranoia*, which means you never rest on your laurels. Because even when you're enjoying success, you always know that the industry and our clients' needs are constantly evolving. As a business owner and leader in general, you should always be striving to improve.

All of that does not leave a lot of time to proactively think about nurturing the company culture. But taking your eyes off the road for even a short time leaves room for miscommunication, discontent, and conflict. You'll find that left unchecked, the culture you've spent so much time and energy creating can quickly dissolve into an unhealthy, unhappy environment. Unhappiness leads to employee turnover. Turnover leads to inefficiency and lost revenue.

Heart culture starts and ends at the top, and it's up to you to be persistent in your efforts to cultivate and maintain a healthy heart culture. What follows are four tips to help you maintain relationships (and reinforce your culture) with your employees.

Choose the Right Management Team

It's not possible for a leader to be everywhere all the time, and that's why a strong, unified management team is the best offense when maintaining a healthy heart culture. What do I look for in a leader? Someone who is a good listener and communicator/facilitator, someone who is diplomatic and respectful, and, overall, someone who is inclusive of everyone on the team. That is, someone who reflects and lives the values of the firm.

I am very much a team player. A command-and-control type of structure is not how I operate, and in my experience it is not the most effective method of leading a team. I believe a good leader has to be open to ideas and be okay with saying, "Your idea is better than mine." That kind of confidence comes from having people around you who are closer to the work and who at the same time are creative and passionate and share the firm's goals. I believe that everybody has a voice worth hearing, and often the best feedback I receive comes from the trenches. My management team works with different departments that I don't necessarily have as much exposure to, and these managers give me information that helps me make better decisions while considering the rest of the staff.

For example, when a manager said to me that I needed to empower a team lead to recruit new hires for her department, I had to absorb this advice while considering the ramifications for the rest of the team. I asked, "What are the company's priorities for hiring? Which departments are shorthanded—and who might possibly be sensitive to my allowing one team but not another to recruit new hires? What do I need to communicate to the firm that ensures everyone understands our current hiring plans and our future plans?"

With the right management team in place I can see into all departments, and in this particular situation, I could discuss with other leaders the impact one new hire could have on the firm's culture. If that seems tedious, trust me, it can be. But focusing on maintaining open and honest communication while protecting culture means less likelihood of pushback and employee dissatisfaction.

My responsibility as a leader is to support people to be the best they can be while also considering the needs of the rest of the firm. My management team is an extension of that role, and I rely on them to help me bridge the gaps and overcome barriers that could be hindering our success.

Don't Wait for a Scheduled Meeting to Check In

Think you need a scheduled one-on-one to check in with individual employees or to give praise? Just a couple of weeks ago, I was thinking about how well a certain client meeting had gone, and, in particular, how well a young planner in my firm had handled the client. He had been at my firm for just a year but I was impressed with his communication and client services skills. So I picked up the phone and left him a voice-mail message on his cell. It went something like this:

> Hi, John [not his real name], it's Greg. Sorry to bother you this late on a Friday, but I just wanted to leave you a message. I was thinking of you and what

a great job you did today, and how appreciative I am that you've chosen to work at Private Ocean. You bring a lot to the team! Anyway, you don't need to call me back. Just let me know if there's anything I can do for you. Have a great weekend!

No, that wasn't a script. It was genuinely how I felt at the moment, and I thought I did not need to wait for our next one-on-one to share my appreciation. On Monday morning, he popped his head into my office and asked if I had a moment.

He was a little surprised by the voicemail, because he wasn't sure if there was an ulterior motive—something he was missing or not reading between the lines. That's the culture he and many of us are more familiar with in a corporate environment. But then he guessed that I did that for a lot of people and that I didn't randomly reach out to keep employees on their toes.

I laughed a bit, but then confirmed his suspicions. I let him know then that while I have reminders on my calendar to call employees for birthdays and work anniversaries, I don't wait for scheduled times or special occasions to let anyone know that they've done a good job. I reiterated my stance on his management of the client meeting, and told him that I wanted to remind him right then that he was appreciated and respected for his work.

That's not just good leadership, it is human nature. Work without any personal connection or caring is just work, and who wants that 40-plus hours a week? When I walk down the hall or pass by the lunchroom at Private Ocean, I stop by and say hello to people and interact with those who I don't always see. When I travel back to Raleigh to Junxure, I make it a point to stop by every single desk to say hello to the employee working there.

At both companies I take a moment to ask employees how things are going for them at work and in their lives. I talk about family, work, and even upcoming company events that are designed to shake up the usual nine-to-five. These are basic human interactions that help foster a personal connection that expands into how well we work together.

With my employees, I try to understand and know their personalities, their goals, and what matters most to them. At Junxure, these brief conversations remind them that the 3,000-mile distance from San Francisco to Raleigh is insignificant when it comes to relationships based on mutual respect and caring.

You cannot say to your employees often enough that your door is open to talk. A leader has to prove it by meeting people more than halfway so they feel as well as think that you are serious about encouraging them to talk.

That being said, it's important that while encouraging any-time communication leaders not dismiss regularly scheduled check-ins with teams and individual employees. Structure is good, and having periodic meetings to discuss not just the firm but also the employee's evolving ideas, concerns, and challenges is always a positive endeavor.

Where do these meetings go wrong? A regularly scheduled check-in requires that the leader be prepared. Too often a leader has not taken the time to review notes from the previous meeting, reread recent emails from the employee, and think about topics that are going to drive a productive conversation. In the absence of this simple preparation, regularly scheduled check-ins will devolve into nothing more than status updates and leave the employee feeling unimportant and thinking that the meeting is just for your needs rather than really wanting to check in with him.

These regular meetings should be productive and support both the leader and the employee. They should also serve as mentoring sessions in which you can share your experiences and help build the leadership skills that can take an employee beyond client management into practice management, especially as you consider future leaders of your firm.

Empower Individuals Regularly, Giving Them the Tools They Need to Succeed—Delegate

Delegation is tough for leaders because it means letting go of the reins and allowing other people to make decisions on behalf of the company.

In an investment firm, especially one that an advisor has built from the ground up, it takes a lot of time to build enough trust to let go and empower individuals. Leaders still struggle with giving up the command-and-control leadership model in which a CEO's fingerprint can be found on every decision in the firm. But that just does not work as effectively in today's market; being responsible for every decision made in the firm simply is not the best or most productive use of a leader's time.

When you don't empower the people you hired to take care of your business, you also risk losing out on new ideas and the best performance of employees you hired to do more than be your yes people.

With respect to new employees today, a leader's job should be to equip them with the tools, knowledge, and guidance necessary to be successful in managing your firm. But then you have to do something unimaginable. *You have to allow them to participate.*

Does that mean your employees get carte blanche to wield decision-making power over the firm? Of course not. You will always have the final say (in my experience it will be necessary at times to intervene and make the final decision). But knowing your company is in good hands, with people who share your values and goals, ultimately gives you peace of mind that you've done something right.

A recent example came from our director of consulting and training for the technology company, who was looking ahead at the future of customer training. In our discussion I asked, "If you could look into a crystal ball, what would you envision as the best possible service that would be beneficial to both the firm and our customers?" After some thought, she laid out an incredible e-learning portal, which would take a considerable investment of time and money but in the end position us at the forefront of technology and service. I was thrilled by the possibilities before us, and without her knowledge of the industry and our customers I would have never considered that path.

In the end, she felt empowered to move the needle and I felt incredibly grateful to have her on the team; it's a reminder to me that hiring the right people makes all the difference in a firm, no matter its size or history.

Plan Regular Off-Site Events for Team Building

Off-site events don't come cheap; that's a fact. But the downside of skipping them is that you miss out on crucial team-building opportunities: relationship-building time that can bridge communication gaps and resolve growing conflict in a day instead of six months.

Company events are often planned to boost morale and bring a group together, and to have some fun—two very noble pursuits. They also facilitate communication and break down barriers between individuals in the firm. And as the team's leader, part of the planning that goes into these events should be based on your intuition about the company's current situation and how employees are feeling. A few events that have really been successful for my firms over the years follow.

The Customer Service Experiment

At my investment advisory firm I wanted to both reward my team for all of its hard work and give it an idea of how I envisioned thinking about client service—where *clients* included our fellow colleagues.

At the time we were a small firm of five people who had dedicated years to helping our clients. To reward ourselves, I set up an overnight stay at the Ritz-Carlton in San Francisco and stipulated just a few guidelines to my employees. They had to attend the dinner that night with the group—this was not an issue as we had a blast together. But they also had to spend $100 at the hotel on a service, and they had to utilize the concierge for something. I also asked them to keep their eye on customer service and how the Ritz-Carlton staff treats its customers, and to take notice of how they felt and what they experienced when interacting with the hotel staff. The following Monday we had a debriefing meeting that sparked a very interesting discussion about what the notion *being appreciated* meant to different people. One employee mentioned a Ritz-Carlton staff person who was in the middle of washing windows yet stopped and asked about how the employee was enjoying his stay. She also asked if there was anything she could do to help.

Was it this woman's job to inquire about customer satisfaction? The answer, the group decided, was yes. Because no matter what your role is in a firm, your goal—our goal—is to make our clients happy. That was a powerful takeaway for the group, who left feeling appreciated with a renewed sense of their purpose in the firm.

CUSTOMER SERVICE AND EMPLOYEE EMPOWERMENT

Ritz-Carlton hotels are known for their incredible customer service, and have publicized that each of its employees may spend up to $2,000 per incident to resolve a customer issue.

Empowering employees to deliver great customer service is key to the success of a business. Don't think so? Then consider this—the average Ritz-Carlton customer will spend $250,000 with the company over his or her lifetime.

The Luxury Bus

Another example of a successful off-site event we planned happened at Junxure and is still referred to as The Bus. We were still a small, growing company—a team of about 15 employees—and at the end of the Friday before our Saturday retreat I had a giant luxury bus pick us up at the office in Raleigh. Before we left for dinner, surrounded by many empty seats, I got up and asked everyone to take notice of how many seats were around them. I wanted them to understand that we were all on an exciting journey together and that someday soon every one of those seats would be filled with someone who was as dedicated and passionate about the company as they were. Junxure was thinking big—bigger than just 15 people in a small office in Raleigh—and everyone present was part of something very special. The bus itself was also symbolic in that it represented the kind of company we viewed ourselves as, and the type of service our customers expected of us. Nowadays, during the hiring process, I often hear from employees that we're "just waiting for the right person to sit on the bus with us."

The Family Weekend

The family weekend off-site event was planned after my firm merger, when we were still developing a new culture and bridging communication gaps.

My firm was a small boutique practice that managed about $250 million in assets. Our model was to lead with financial planning and charge up-front planning fees while also providing investment management, all with a very high-service, high-touch model. The firm we merged with was twice the size with nearly twice the money under management and a model that focused more on academic investment expertise than financial planning, but that also provided clients a high level of service.

Despite the differences, where the two firms aligned was in our philosophy to service our clients, our ideas for growth versus scale, and our vision to go with an internal succession plan for the company.

One memorable trip we planned early on—as a way to help build relationships—was a cabin vacation on a river near the office. We invited all employees and their families to spend a summer weekend together in a very casual setting that was meant to help set the tone for how we wanted to work together—as a family.

We organized a team-building dinner that incorporated friendly competition among different groups that were responsible for preparing parts of the meal. Want to get to know your employees and see how well people work together? Assign them the task of making appetizers for 40 people and pit them against the dessert team.

When you get people outside of their work environments you get to see them in their element. You learn things about them and their families that you would not have ever known otherwise. And employees who may be gun-shy about meeting with their leaders have ample opportunity to gain one-on-one time that can be both casual and unscheduled.

That weekend we ate huge buffet meals, played in Ping-Pong competitions, and enjoyed all kinds of sports and activities. People played and participated or simply watched from the sidelines—whatever they felt most comfortable doing. It was very important to me that no one felt forced to play. And all fun aside, our goal in this activity was to create opportunities to build relationships between people, foster new friendships and solidify existing ones, and break down communication barriers or misunderstandings that can build up day after day when all you do is work nine to five together. It's analogous to the Tin Man from *The Wizard of Oz*: If you don't tend to the joints, if you're lazy and dismiss the warning signs of rust, the machine starts to become less flexible and adaptable.

These types of outings and events are amazing at fostering teamwork, collaboration, and open communication. They encourage positive relationships and, on top of everything else, are just plain fun.

The family picnic was so successful that we have continued it to this day, and it's amazing to see how much people look forward to the weekend together.

A lot of time is taken with planning these events and making them memorable because I know the lasting impact they have on employees. I get inspired by how delivering a message effectively means more than getting people to understand what you're trying to accomplish. It means getting them to *feel* the way you do about a certain goal or initiative.

Each event, each retreat, and each team-building event is different. Therefore a lot goes into making sure that each time we gather together there is a theme that relates to how the company and its people are feeling at that moment. The result of a carefully executed company event is that employees leave with a reinforced belief in its management team, in the company, and in the direction we're all headed together.

Once you've gathered all of this information and discussed the theme and agenda with your management team, your facilitator can develop an agenda that can be reviewed and modified as needed. To-do items are then assigned to leaders and teams to prepare. Don't be married to the script, though, as things tend to change all the time in our business. Always be prepared to make a last-minute change as things come up.

Client Appreciation Events

Client appreciation events are an often-overlooked team-building opportunity that can help bring your team closer together. The loyalty that you can build through picnics, parties, and dinners for clients is also rewarding and validating for your employees' hard work. These events also help build personal connections between your team and your clients and can even lead to new business. We've found that our team looks forward to these gatherings as much as our clients do each year.

At Private Ocean, our company picnic has reached somewhat legendary status. We've continuously upped the ante, too: what began as a small gathering in a park is now a full-fledged celebration at a winery with entertainment, food, and even face painting and exotic animals for the kids. This past year we had almost 200 people attend, including our staff and their families.

Client appreciation events are a worthwhile investment not only in your clients but also in the well-being of your firm.

The Company Retreat

In addition to the team-building events held during the year, every January we kick off the year with a company retreat. For Private Ocean, we have a two-day event off-site. This event is meant to set the tone for the coming year and to look back and acknowledge all of the hard work of the previous year.

Our basic template for the retreat goes like this:

- **An update on the business ("state of the state").** The update includes stats on how we stack up against our goals, what our plans are for the year, and why we believe we can achieve them. It is also very important to review the vision for the company—that is, where are we heading?

- **Report out from all departments.** This is a quick, three-to-five-minute presentation with the guidelines that each department review what it accomplished the previous year and what it's planning for that year. The teams show great creativity in their presentations to make them informative and entertaining!

- **Fireside chats.** This is a Q&A session with leaders responding to anything that may be on the employees' minds, including questions about company vision and strategy.

- **Team-building activities.** We encourage activities that involve teams working together that also have employees interacting with those they may not speak to, or work with, on a regular basis. This helps keep the camaraderie close. This year one of the areas of focus was how to take better care of our clients and increase our service levels, and importantly, how we can reduce client effort in working with us.

- **Recognition and acknowledgment.** The period for recognition and acknowledgment is critical to the company's focus on people before business. We have run this in a number of ways that have all been very impactful on, and positive for, everyone. For example, at one meeting everyone drew a name at the beginning of the day. At the end of the day each person acknowledged the person whose name was drawn for what he saw that person contributing to the company's success—and if he had had personal experiences with that person he could share those.

At Junxure, since much of the company is located remotely across the country, the event takes place over four days at our headquarters in North Carolina.

Junxure Week plays out like this—the management team and department leaders get together throughout the week and talk about the company's strategy for the year. We prioritize, work on ongoing projects and strategy, and generally create the road map of things to come.

For the rest of the employees, the goal is to not cause too much disruption to their daily schedules. Imagine that you work in an office upon which half of the company descends for one week a year. It can be stressful. So we encourage personal interaction, stage company meals, and keep things casual.

On Saturday we hold an all-day retreat to bring it all together. This is when I bring in our executive coach to facilitate the day's activities, which follow a similar agenda to our Private Ocean retreats. The difference is that we focus even more on team-building activities that help us bridge communication gaps, since we don't often see one another face-to-face.

Take for example a recent Junxure company retreat. The previous year had been a challenging one, with many of our efforts dedicated to the final stages of development, testing, and releasing Junxure Cloud, a cloud-based CRM solution for advisors that was years in the making.

Every single person on the team worked tirelessly on the project, many of them sacrificing nights, weekends, and even vacations to make sure we put together a product that we would be proud to offer our customers. That dedication and pride are some of the best parts of our culture, and the weeks leading up to this retreat were emotional. We felt in many ways that we had reached a finish line together.

So when planning for the event, the leadership team took into account the general state of the company's morale. We all felt that the tone was that of inspiration, hope, and appreciation of one another—but also, well, fatigue. So we used all of that for the retreat's theme: recognition and gratitude.

Instead of the usual action-packed schedule and team-building activities, the entire event's agenda was planned around recognizing individuals as well as teams and calling out accomplishments. We upgraded the venue and handed out prizes. We served food, played games, and encouraged camaraderie by establishing a more laid-back vibe.

The feedback I received after the retreat was overwhelmingly positive. People who had felt discouraged by the hard road now felt a renewed sense of hope, and those who had felt overlooked realized that they were, indeed, appreciated. In just two days we reset the company's morale and reinvigorated its people. That is the power of a company retreat for your culture.

Get Started Planning a Company Retreat: Five Questions

If planning a retreat seems daunting, keep in mind these five questions that can help you lay the groundwork for a successful and effective event. Remember, always work backward with the end in mind!

1. **What do you want to achieve?** The first step in planning a company retreat is to consider your desired high-level outcomes. How do you want everyone to feel when leaving the meeting? Do you want to boost morale? Improve employee loyalty? Get everyone back on the same page after a tough year? Clearly lay out next year's strategy? First and foremost you should have the end in mind—what do you want people to leave with? Once you have your list, share it with your leadership team and facilitator and talk as a group about what you want to accomplish. In my case I always want people to leave feeling appreciated and also to have a better understanding of where we are as a company— and where we are going. I also want to identify and work on our big issues.

2. **What is the state of the company?** Every company retreat should have a theme based on the current state of the company or the industry. The themes will not always be the same, though I think if you're not paying

attention they may all seem the same. In our retreats I always reflect on what the company is currently going through and how it may be affecting employees and the overall culture. I always try to stay attuned to what people are feeling. In 2009, for example, after a blistering year of economic upheaval, the theme at Private Ocean's retreat was that you cannot control the wind—but you can adjust the sails. Another consideration with regard to the state of the company is growth. Has the company changed structurally? Have you added key positions of leadership or perhaps a new department? Make sure you plan for a retreat that accommodates the company. A lot can change in a short time.

3. **What topics do we need to address?** Once you have identified your desired outcomes and decided on a theme, then you can take the planning a level deeper and drill down to specific topics you and your management team want to address. I also welcome feedback from everyone in the firm and ask for topics they'd like us to cover, as well as what *they* would like to accomplish and address at the meeting.

4. **Where should we have the event?** The location of your retreat is just as important as the material you intend to cover. For example, in my firms we always hold these retreats off-site because we don't want interruptions and distractions, and we intentionally want to break up the routine people expect in the workplace. We also take this opportunity to go to nicer hotels or venues, where people can feel comfortable and relaxed. The location definitely plays a part in supporting what we want to achieve.

5. **What format should we use?** I have held company retreats for years, and at this point we have several key components that make up the morning's activities. This helps us set a certain expectation that people will get the information they expect from the leaders. We begin with a state-of-the-state component and update everyone on goals, company results, and our action plan for the year. We then include some form of acknowledgment— taking stock of what we've done as a company histori- cally as well as acknowledging all the things that were accomplished in the last year. We incorporate team reports, giving each department a short period of time to quickly report on its accomplishments and goals for the future. Then we make sure to include a leadership Q&A—a free forum that gives employees the chance to ask any question they have of their leaders. Then we consider the afternoon activities, which are usually very different from retreat to retreat. This is where we use activities, games, and presentations to help promote our theme, which is ultimately to work on business issues and come up with tactics for hitting goals for the year.

Persistence and Consistency Recap: Tips to Remember

- Your management team must be in alignment with your goals and in tune with your culture. Your managers are your eyes and ears as well as your ambassadors of culture!

- Don't put off until tomorrow what you can take care of today! Don't wait for a regularly scheduled check-in with an employee to address an issue.
- Good leaders delegate! Your job is to equip your employees with the right tools, knowledge, and guidance necessary to be successful in managing your firm.
- Take advantage of off-site team-building events. Getting everyone outside of the office is not only refreshing, it quickly breaks down barriers and helps motivate people to get to know one another and understand one another's needs. These events can also be a great way to deliver a message.

Benefits

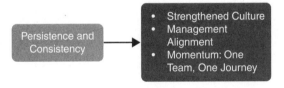

Chapter 6

Encouragement

*Rewarding Firm-Wide Collaboration
and a Team Mentality*

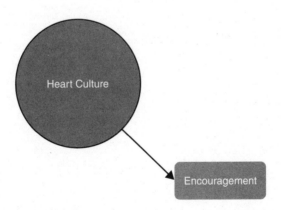

A company with a strong sense of teamwork and collaboration can move mountains together. Culture plays a key role in establishing that

one-for-all mentality, so it's up to you to set up parameters that encourage people to want to work together.

How does a leader encourage collaboration in a heart culture? By following these five key steps:

1. Reiterating company values
2. Creating individual opportunities
3. Rewarding teamwork through the compensation structure
4. Keeping people accountable—even yourself
5. Holding a biannual company retreat

Reiterating Company Values

In my experience it's fairly common for a company to give the mission-and-philosophy speech just once—during the required orientation session that new hires go through in their first week of employment. Besides that, they're lucky to get a handout in the employee manual that glosses over the company's beliefs, which they can hang in their work spaces.

I don't consider that approach terribly inspiring or effective if you're trying to build and nurture a culture based on respect, open communication, collegiality, and hard work. Words on paper mean very little unless they are backed up by actions.

Hiring the right people is part of the solution: Positive, inspiring, hardworking people who believe in the company's values are powerful messengers. But you cannot just rely on others to carry and reiterate your message. It's important for leaders to always keep the firm's values front and center during every company meeting and in every conversation between their management team and their employees.

If open communication is valuable to you and your culture (and it should be!), set the example by always making the point that even as a leader you share as much information as possible with your members of your team so that they feel included and informed. If you want to encourage collaboration, create the environment for people to work together effectively, and ask for feedback and ideas along the way.

You can never overcommunicate your values with words or with actions, so be sure to take every opportunity possible to remind your team that your mission statement and your values are more than just words.

Creating Individual Opportunities

Sometimes when leaders set individual goals and incentives for employees they inadvertently create a competitive environment that walks the line between encouraging success and creating conflict. If you want people to act like a team they should want to succeed as one.

Working together successfully means building relationships with our coworkers that are based on mutual care and respect. Choosing the right people for the job is absolutely important (see Chapter 1, "Patience"), but once you're all on The Bus together you need to believe that your coworkers want you to succeed and that they're willing to help you on your way *and* on our way to success. And when people genuinely support you, this support removes that instinctively defensive edge. You feel encouraged and empowered, and in return you want to support others in their endeavors.

A good example of the collaborative work environment I feel we've truly succeeded in building in both my companies is that no one is afraid to ask for help. People take a lot of pride in what they do, and they are appreciated and acknowledged for their skills. Everyone fits together in a way that most benefits our clients—who are always our first priority. So when employees ask for help from someone, there is no hesitation about sharing knowledge.

Does this mean no one's busy or has a specific job to do? Absolutely not. But our job is to help others, and every person has a lot of passion about doing great work for clients. We have built a culture that says, "We are all in this together. We are all one part of something great that—when put together—can truly make a difference in people's lives." Everybody is necessary and each member of our team plays a role in our success. We are one big team.

Rewarding Teamwork through the Compensation Structure

A key component of encouraging collaboration is to weave team-centric goals into employee compensation (including bonuses and incentives).

In addition to individual goals teams should have overall goals that require them to work together to succeed. These can be by department. For example, at Private Ocean, we're adopting a rebalancing system, and we've got over 400 clients and families that need to be converted into this new system. Our investment operations team has set a goal of having all clients moved within 12 months, and it has created a roadmap to achieve this goal. Incentives can also be by company—for example, if the firm reaches certain financial goals, the team receives a year-end bonus.

These kinds of goals encourage people to work together, and that incentive produces new ideas and developments that are supported and promoted by the entire group. Credit is given where credit is due. I think of this approach as lifting everyone up instead of keeping people down—one person's success does not come at the expense of another's.

In contrast, I have seen environments that have been competitive to an extent that is just not productive. You may have some high-producing rock stars willing to step on the backs of others to make the company lots of money in the short term, but do you think this type of hypercompetitive environment encourages loyalty? Trust? Longevity?

Speaking of longevity, even a company that has a healthy heart culture experiences ups and downs when it comes to turnover. It's one of the costs of focusing on and encouraging individuals to follow their own paths. The truth is that sometimes, the employee's path simply is not with your firm.

Your responsibility as a leader isn't to count the losses, because there will be a few, but to continue maintaining a collaborative, caring culture for the majority of employees who continue to stay with the company.

Jane: The Noncollaborative Leader

After college graduation, I transferred to the corporate offices of a large retailer in a new position—reorder specialist in the purchasing department —that came with a very specific job description and a set list of tasks. In that department no one was encouraging me to think about the good of the company or to even think outside the lines of my specific assignments. My leader at the time, Jane (not her real name), was deeply insecure about her position and very concerned about how her superiors viewed her, wanting nothing more than for her employees to do exactly as they were told and to not overstep the bounds of their job descriptions. In fact, she made sure we were virtually invisible to her superiors and took credit for any successes we had, regardless of who actually contributed to them.

Because of her leadership approach and management style, the culture, morale, and overall environment there were depressing and not at all motivating. I used to hate going into the office. I remember pulling into the parking lot on Monday mornings and giving myself a pep talk just so that I could get through the week.

The work I was allowed to do wasn't particularly challenging or time consuming, and there was a set amount of work to do each week. As I am not one to waste time or procrastinate, I would often get my work done early in the week. My coworkers would tell me that I needed to pace myself, as they purposely did, slowing their pace to make the work last all week. That way they could keep their easy jobs, appease our insecure leader, and not draw any unnecessary attention to themselves.

Each week I generally finished my workload by Wednesday afternoon. That wasn't going to work for me, so I went to Jane and asked for more responsibilities. She said no, as I was hired to perform a specific set of tasks and "not qualified" by virtue of my job to do any more. That was discouraging, but since I am not the type to sit still, I started to come up with ideas in my free time.

Using my experience from working in the warehouse at my previous company, I suggested ways to do some things differently that could save money and make for a more efficient process for the company. I explained this to Jane, but she was not only uninterested in my ideas, but also annoyed that I was clearly stepping beyond my job description.

I was disappointed because I had a sense of loyalty for this company and I genuinely cared for its people and its success. So instead of accepting her dismissal, I took a chance and submitted my proposal to her superiors.

What did this mean for my relationship with Jane? Obviously she was furious with me and she did all she could to make her displeasure with me clear. It was not very long after that I transferred to another department within the company and eventually decided to pursue financial planning as a career.

Team versus Machine

What my experiences with poor leadership led to was my desire to be a leader who treated people the way I wanted to be treated—as someone respected and listened to. I wanted to be a leader who was much more open to voices and new ideas. When there are restrictions and barriers to productivity in the workplace, it implies a fundamental lack of respect that can lead to an environment of fear. Jane, I realized much later, was simply insecure. Ideas that did not come from her were considered a threat, so she squashed them before they could be heard and considered. But an effective leader understands that the more you can empower people to think outside the box, the more the company stands to gain from the best ideas. You don't need to micromanage and control every detail of an employee's workday if you hire strong, bright, dedicated people who share your values. A good leader should encourage people to share their ideas and give them the opportunity to feel as if they are part of a team, not a machine. A team has heart. A machine does not.

Keeping People Accountable—Even Yourself

Accountability goes hand in hand with integrity. When you say you're going to do something or that you believe or support something, you are expected to follow through with actions that support your words.

Good intentions may count for something in a heart culture, but ensuring that your employees have a thriving, collaborative work environment means everyone has to pull their weight. Everyone has to meet the same expectations and standards of performance. That means leaders, too.

When it comes to accountability, a leader should look inward before looking outward. Are you living up to your mission statement? Are your actions aligned with your philosophy on business, service, and culture? What kind of example are you setting when it comes to keeping your word and delivering on your promises?

In the wealth management industry (as in any industry), doing what you say you will do is critical. When beginning to work with new clients you make promises and create expectations as to what you will do for them, how you will do it, and how quickly. You share your values and confirm that they are in line with the client's. In other words, expectations are created with clients about the work you will do—the quality and the timeliness—and that it is as important to you as it is to them.

This philosophy applies to the relationship between the leader and the employee as well. When a new hire comes on board, you set expectations that measure success. You also share your values and philosophy on how to work together. You monitor that employee and check in to make sure he has what he needs to meet his goals. As a leader your job is to support your people and encourage them to come to you should they need help. But at the end of the day, that employee is responsible for getting his job done.

Holding people accountable is critical in this leadership model. You can care and you can be understanding and patient, but people still have to perform.

I had a situation in my firm in which an employee had clear expectations of his goals, and though his heart was in the right place and his attitude was positive, his performance wasn't up to par with what we required. This employee didn't communicate well, didn't delegate tasks when it would have been helpful, and wasn't an effective collaborator. It seemed this employee's biggest issue was that he simply wasn't able to manage projects effectively.

While the firm doesn't have a formal code of conduct, expectations for performance and communication are set on an employee's first day and then reinforced in nearly everything we do. Culture is what happens when you're not looking, and in this situation, we had someone who wasn't committing to the values of the company.

To help resolve the issue I had regular check-in meetings to monitor and assess the situation. I encouraged an open dialogue that would have given this employee ample opportunity to ask for help. Instead I consistently got a sugarcoated "everything is fine." Meanwhile his coworkers had started to share feedback on their issues with this employee and how it impacted their work and ability to succeed. It was taking a toll on morale and causing frustration that others had to put in extra time to correct what this one person was doing wrong.

What I was hearing seemed like fixable problems, so I encouraged this person's teammates to attempt to highlight the issue with him constructively and help when they could to make sure he understood what was and wasn't getting done. Some examples of this included:

- Identifying recurring communication issues and potential resolutions that they brought up candidly with the employee.
- Applying their own skill sets in situations in which they might help overcome a workflow obstacle—someone with project management experience, for example, could offer insight to this employee, who struggled to manage tasks assigned to his colleagues.

I saw this situation as a leadership opportunity for this employee's coworkers and asked that these people keep me posted on their progress.

Stepping up has never been an issue in either of my companies, and these people worked hard to help resolve some of the problems, which did indeed get better over time. But at what expense? The time of many others who had to intervene and help correct the mistakes of this one person. And all the while I was hearing from this employee that everything was fine. Well, it was not acceptable, and finally it needed to be addressed.

Clearly I was not pleased, and I explained to him what I knew of the current situation. I knew how much others had helped him along when he was struggling, and I also reminded him of the many occasions he had the opportunity to speak up and ask for help from me. I said to him that the passion I was exhibiting right then was the same passion that I had for doing the right thing for our clients. He was not meeting expectations, he was not following the code of conduct that we expected from our employees, and he was not delivering on his promises. This was a hard conversation to have, but it was a good one. Expectations were reset and there would be no mistaking what this employee needed to do to remain a part of the team in the future. As a result of this conversation the employee changed his way of communicating, and above all, reached out for help when necessary.

In some cases, unfortunately, even an intervention doesn't resolve the issue and it's important to know when it's time to part ways with an employee. In one situation, we had a very bright, capable, and well-liked person who simply did not perform. After a number of conversations that included addressing the issue, setting expectations, and reaching agreements, this person did not improve. Ultimately, we severed the relationship as it was no longer beneficial to the firm or the employee.

In these situations, start by asking questions to assess the situation. Offer support and clearly communicate your expectations for success. You'll find that many employees get this right out of the gate, while others need help and an explanation of what they need to accomplish.

Holding a Biannual Retreat

I spoke in some detail about our firms' company retreats and the impact they have had on our culture. Whether or not you lead a small team in one office, or, like me, manage different groups of people in different locations, the team-building activity or event is important to bringing people together and reminding them why they chose to work for your company in the first place. Team-building events—if done right—can overcome communication challenges, break down boundaries, resolve conflict, and reignite the collaborative energy that can get lost in the day-to-day workplace. They are also very influential in setting a course for a brand-new firm that results from a merger or acquisition.

For instance, years ago when my firm merged with another to form Private Ocean we were faced with two different corporate cultures suddenly fused together. Our firms were built upon a foundation of shared basic values and philosophies on client services and financial planning, but a lot was different. Our communication styles and our approaches to collaboration and how to facilitate it were not yet aligned. While we covered these key topics, the entire event provided a venue to show the joint leadership team's commitment—encouragement—to the joint endeavor.

As you can imagine, the first few company retreats were challenging, and it took a lot of dedication, passion, trust, and hard work to build what would eventually lead to a more cohesive unit. There were lots of tiny issues to bring out and discuss, as well as issues that interfered with getting work done for which it was vital to get on the same page. What is financial planning? What does client services mean? How do we approach technology? In some respects it was like starting a business from the ground floor. We brought in an executive coach to facilitate the event; we needed someone asking all the right questions and helping us navigate these new waters.

Now I know that there are many firms that don't invest in team-building activities such as company retreats, and I think that's a missed opportunity. Because no matter how challenging these first events were for the firm, the outcome was incredibly useful and spoke volumes about our commitment to making this merger work. And going forward, when a particular meeting is painful or gets heated during discussions, this is an instant indicator to me that there is an issue that needs resolution. It provides a unique opportunity for leaders to surface a lot of things that they may not necessarily be exposed to, such as staffing needs, for instance. Sometimes what it takes to unearth these problems is to get a group of people off site, face-to-face, to talk about their questions and concerns.

I am in the unique position of seeing the perspective of two different companies, and it's allowed me to experience both cultures. It's a good gauge because I have seen what a strong heart culture can accomplish, and I simultaneously experience all of the hard work it takes to get there. In the end, I know that all the bumps are worth the smoother road ahead.

There will be ups and downs and your company retreat should reflect what's going on around you and offer an in-person opportunity to deliver encouragement and open and honest dialogue. It's a chance to get out of the office and be in a different environment and focus on the big issues. Don't try to keep it business as usual, because in reality, it's never business as usual.

How often should you hold a company retreat or off-site event? In my opinion twice a year is optimal, with at least one if not two days dedicated to the event. In both my firms we do an annual kick-off meeting in January, and at midyear we do a scaled-down version that's a check-in on goals and projects to make sure we're all still on the same path.

Why two days? The first day is meant to set a positive, constructive tone for the event and set the stage for working *on* the business. The goal is to get people to engage and define the key opportunity areas, and it's more productive to begin by talking about accomplishments and recognizing people for what they have done, and then laying out the plan for the big picture going forward. The second day is when you truly begin to make progress, drilling down on individual and department goals and action plans and what it will take to accomplish these objectives. At the end of the second day, people feel appreciated, engaged, inspired, and clear on their next steps.

All of this work is a key component to creating and maintaining a healthy heart culture. Is it a commitment? Yes—an incredible one that takes perseverance, patience, and tolerance. But I can attest to the power of the right culture when I reflect back on a recent retreat at Private Ocean after years of hard work building relationships and coming together as a group. We now feel like one united team; we have the right people thinking the same way together about the firm, its people, and our future. It was an amazing and empowering event.

Encouragement Recap: Tips to Remember

- Never, ever stop repeating your firm's philosophy and core values.
- Always be sure your actions reflect your values—*walk the walk!*
- Recognize individuals for their unique skills by offering opportunities to grow.
- Encourage teamwork over competition by setting team-based quarterly goals.
- With respect to accountability, look inward first—ask yourself what kind of example you're setting in the firm.
- Consider biannual company retreats that are focused on resetting the sails and bringing the team together.

Benefits

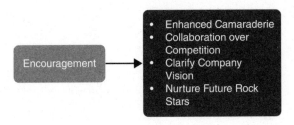

Chapter 7

Courage

Reshaping Your Company's DNA to Establish Heart Culture

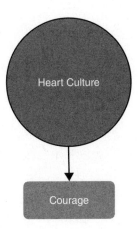

I am frequently asked how I manage to lead and be a part of two successful companies. I always say that it is two things: It is the great people who I work with, and it is making the conscious choice to care—really care. And once you commit to this path you will need to prepare for how that change will impact your work environment and your staff.

Of course, it's one thing to give advice about how a leader should lead with the heart. It's quite another to turn a frigate around that's firmly lodged into an iceberg. Change never happens overnight (not the good, lasting kind, anyway), so perseverance—and courage—plays a hefty part in this process. Here are some first steps I took that helped me get started in realizing my vision of leadership. They are also things I do even today to constantly assess my success as a leader.

1. **I looked at myself.** Before you can assess your corporate culture, you need to look inward. What kind of leader do you want to be? It's important in all aspects of your life to be genuine and honest with yourself. Do you even *want* to be a leader? There are people who identify themselves as owners of companies, not leaders, and they bring in the right people to help them succeed.

   Once you've decided what kind of leader you want to be, ask yourself questions such as: "How am I perceived by employees? How do I handle day-to-day issues? Crisis?" When something negative happens in the company, before I get angry—and anger is a completely necessary emotion sometimes—I ask, "What was my role in this issue? How did I contribute to this situation?" This self-assessment method has completely changed how I approach situations.

I also recommend that leaders read every book they can get their hands on. I have read books that don't resonate at all with me, but I still get something from them. When you're trying to understand the kind of leader you are and want to be, it can only help to do your research and pick up invaluable tips.

2. **I looked at my company.** Once I had a better understanding of my leadership style and its impact on the firm, I started to take stock of the current company culture. Some of the questions I asked myself were:

- What is the current climate of the firm and what is impacting the environment?
- How is morale at the firm and how in tune to it am I as a leader?
- Are people happy to be here? What does happiness look like?
- How well do we communicate across teams? With leadership?
- How are individuals recognized for their accomplishments?
- How well do we collaborate across teams?

A few years ago, we did a company exercise in which everyone introduced themselves, talked a little about their backgrounds, and shared what their roles were. One employee, who was relatively new to the company and was hired in a very key—and senior—role, stood up and announced dismissively that she was unsure of what her role was in the company. This was because she was used to working in environments that were very hierarchical and not collaborative, and she wasn't getting her way—and was *not* happy about this. This was her way of letting me and others know. The negative impact of that one comment shifted the atmosphere in the room—here was an obviously key person acting out. At 5:01 p.m. she was dismissed, and the team was notified the next day. I did this for two reasons: She obviously was not a cultural fit with the firm and was going to be an obstruction in achieving our goals, and I wanted to send the entire firm a message that this behavior is not acceptable and would not be tolerated.

Asking yourself these basic questions can help you gauge how wide the gap is between your current culture and the one you envision. Making swift changes isn't always easy, but once you have a clear vision of your ideal corporate culture, it's never too early to get started.

3. **I hired an executive coach to work with me and to help bring it together.** I cannot stress enough the benefits I have received from having an outside voice—one trained to assess leadership success—to help me in my business: an executive coach, who will tell you directly what you *need* to hear. Why should you hire a coach? Look at professional athletes. They work with coaches every day who assess their current situations and help them improve. I have worked with several executive coaches in my career, and each one has contributed to my success. My current executive coach of many years, Sharon Hoover, has helped me in many ways, from bridging communication gaps to understanding conflict to cultivating a collaborative spirit in both my firms.

CRITERIA FOR HIRING AN EXECUTIVE COACH

Here are a few things to consider when looking for an executive coach:

- **You have to be coachable.** You have to be willing to have people tell you things and be willing to change.
- **Get references from your peers and ask questions.** "What does this person do for you? How does she work for you? What kind of things do you work on?" For example, there are business-oriented coaches who are focused on your career goals and there are life coaches who are focused on helping you set and achieve personal goals. Both can be amazingly valuable and effective in business and in life.
- **Interview a few of them.** Don't be afraid to work with one for a period of time before switching to a new coach. Each one has different skills and tools to help you achieve your goals, which evolve over time. I've worked with several coaches and gathered valuable advice from each of them.
- **Consider chemistry.** When you're letting someone into your life you need to make sure he fits with your personality—but be prepared to be challenged.
- **Consider culture.** If you have your coach work with your company you should also consider the cultural match, keeping in mind there's no one right solution for everyone.

Deciding that you want to change your company's culture means thinking about the world—that is, the world beyond your company—in a completely different way. That is no easy feat, so you must take your time as you work through the process of building a strong and successful heart culture.

If you're wondering where you should begin, I always say to start with your personal goals for the firm's healthy culture. Some things to think about are:

- What is your personal idea of a fulfilling work culture?
- What things matter most to you in your career?
- Are you surrounded by the kinds of people who will support you and join you in this endeavor?
- Do their goals and values align with yours?

If you're like me, you got into this business because you wanted to help people to meet their financial and life goals, to live comfortably with peace of mind, and to not outlive their money. Those same basic goals could be applied to you and your staff, but what else do you want to achieve?

It's like I mentioned before, when I spoke about the "dream" speech that I give all new hires. For me, a fulfilling work culture is one in which employees are excited to come in to work because they get to do satisfying, challenging work with people whom they respect and enjoy working with, in an environment where they feel appreciated and recognized.

If you gave *your* "dream" speech today, what would you say? How much would you mean it?

Once you've got a clear picture on your ideal work culture, it's time to take some steps toward making your dream a reality.

Assessing Your Team's Individual Strengths and Opportunities

I have stressed several times in this book how important the right hires and the right people are to your culture's health. There is an art to identifying the right kind of people, who are qualified to do the job you need and who can also sync with the existing culture. The truth is, no matter how efficient an employee is, if she doesn't fit into your culture, no one will be happy.

Most of us aren't in the position, however, to start creating the perfect team from scratch. The reality is you already have a team to work with—a team of people you hopefully respect and care about enough to implement cultural changes that will benefit everyone involved.

One influential exercise to consider is an assessment called the Birkman Method.[1] The Birkman Method is a well-known and well-utilized personality, social perception, and occupational interest assessment consisting of 10 scales describing occupational preferences (interests), 11 scales describing effective behaviors (usual behaviors), and 11 scales describing interpersonal and environmental expectations (needs or expectations). A corresponding set of 11 scale values was derived to describe less than effective behaviors (stress behaviors). The result categorizes each person into the color group by which he or she is most defined:

- **Red:** expediting, with a focus on solving problems
- **Blue:** planning, ideas, and innovation
- **Green:** communication, promoting, and motivating
- **Yellow:** organizing, focused on rules and procedures

This assessment was incredibly helpful at Private Ocean after the merger because it helped us understand how people work together, how they communicate, and how they deal with stress. It also identified the circumstances in which people were at their best, what their capabilities were, and what their strengths were as part of our new team. We didn't consider the assessment a branding or labeling exercise, but rather a great jumping-off point to start asking questions.

For our company retreats back then (and even now) we often "showed our colors" as we took part in an activity wearing our corresponding colors as a reminder of the way in which each one of us works most effectively, including what we wanted and needed in our teammates. The results are always positive, helping us further develop relationships by building trust and breaking down communication barriers.

The Birkman Method has now also become a point of discussion company-wide during the hiring process, as we consider how someone new might integrate into the firm. A lot of what is assessed is about communications and how a particular person interacts with others. Is he a good collaborator? Does she need more direction than others? How does he handle crisis situations and how does he solve problems?

For example, someone in the firm tested as Blue, with a communication style that is very verbose, a preference for strategizing more about the big picture than the details, and an aversion to making sudden decisions. How would this Blue person work with someone who prefers the decisive, straightforward approach to handling a crisis situation of a

Red? These personality assessment tools are very helpful in understanding how people operate and how they'll likely work together. The value in heart leadership is that taking advantage of these additional tools can help you understand what each of your employees needs to succeed and to be happy.

As a leader, you should absolutely take the assessment yourself to understand your own strengths and needs! My results landed me in the Green area, which indicated that my strengths are not "extreme." Rather, my strength—as I have been told on many occasions—is that I can relate to, see, and empathize with all sides involved.

That skill set lends itself to a certain style of leadership that has been very successful for me. I believe that people who lead with a lot of caring and heart can usually understand other people's points of view. Some of that empathy comes from understanding my businesses from the ground up.

We have even done this looking at the leadership team as a group. This has helped us work together with greater understanding.

As a leader, understanding your color as well as the color of others will help you shape your interpersonal skills and communications with other leaders and employees, and help you to be cognizant of where you yourself may be tripped up by other people's motivations and needs. I ask myself, "How do I—as a Green—make sure I don't drive those decisive Reds crazy?"

Recognizing individual strengths and opportunities is every leader's responsibility, so it pays to use the tools available to you in order to help your team work together collaboratively to understand your firm's unique dynamics. No two companies are ever alike, and that mostly comes down to the fact that no two people are exactly alike. Be sure to evaluate, appreciate, and utilize your firm's special DNA to create something special and vital to your culture's health.

Anticipating Growing Pains—Lots of Them

I cannot underscore the importance of striking the right balance between stability and continued growth enough, especially in a market in which the times are always changing. While your business model must adapt to sea changes, what should never change is your disciplined focus on maintaining your company's soul, the spirit of its culture. True success—the rock-solid kind that is sustainable over the long term—is anchored by having a team of efficient self-starters who as a whole share your vision of success and of the firm's future.

Everyone from client services professionals to office managers and senior leaders contributes to the firm's health, and they should be encouraged to participate in the conversation as you chart the course of your future.

Growing pains during these changes—firm growth, economic uncertainty, staff changes, and limited resources—can take a real toll on your culture, especially if you're in the midst of making improvements. Here are some tips to address these challenges:

- **Firm growth.** As your business evolves, it can be challenging to keep some of the little things from falling through the cracks. Did the new advisor get proper training on how to handle client phone calls? Are the newer client services people understanding and tracking activities the way your veteran staff has in the past? Are things getting so busy that response time to clients is increasing? With so many balls in the air it can be hard to manage change appropriately while remaining true to your business model. What's important is to constantly remind the team that the goal is to take care of clients and pay attention to details so that the work gets done the way it needs to get done. Everyone has a responsibility to protect the firm's reputation and values.

- **Economic uncertainty.** Ironically, there is always economic uncertainty. Has there ever been a time when the economy has been certain? For wealth management, as for every other industry, the period between 2008 and 2009 was truly a watershed event. Every day the news was terrible, and every day we had to calm clients and work harder than ever before—while firm revenues fell. At Private Ocean, I'm really proud of how we handled that situation: by actively communicating with clients and one another to get through the toughest of times. As a leader, that meant getting in before sunrise and leaving after sunset and always having the game face on. You don't always have to have the answers right then, but people depend on you to say that things will be okay and that you'll get through whatever situation is placed in front of you. Leaders have to be cheerleaders and show strength and courage, even when faced with the biggest challenges.

My approach also included showing a bit of vulnerability. Why? Because what we needed, in addition to reassurance, was honesty and an acknowledgment that times were tough. We were not necessarily in trouble, but things were troubling. I would update the team daily with where we were and what the plan was to date. I also shared plans B and C. Knowledge can really be powerful, and you have to reinforce your message.

- **Staff changes.** Turnover is inevitable, but how you handle communicating these changes really sets the tone within a company culture. I put a lot of thought into the best way to announce an employee's departure; I want to be candid, honest, and open, yet respectful of the situation at hand. The best approach is to address the change head-on and immediately, to stop rumors from popping up. If the departure is planned, we work with the employee to craft a message so that everyone is on the same page. But when an employee leaves abruptly, I gather everyone together quickly and explain the situation. I share the overall facts, keep things positive, and talk about how we'll move forward. This is especially important in smaller firms where the absence of one person really has an impact on the business.

- **Limited resources.** There are often times when people feel overworked or that their workload is stressful because appropriate resources are lacking. There are certainly things leaders can do about these situations, but sometimes they are simply a product of growth and the business needs time to catch up. I recommend working with employees to set realistic expectations of goals and then encouraging them to think outside the box to help alleviate some of the stress. Empower them to make decisions about getting the things done that are in the interest of the client. Sometimes great ideas come from these situations. Also, support them: They can only do so much, and as long as they are doing all they can, that is all I can ask!

Another issue we've faced at both companies is how we sometimes feel rushed or compromised when it comes to delivering services and products. We are so focused on giving our clients the best service that it sometimes affects the client experience in unintended ways. It's my job to balance the passion that these people have for their work with the company's needs, and to stay focused on the client experience.

Recognizing Culture Killers and How to Avoid Them

You've now got a list of goals and you're armed with some helpful information on everyone you work with. Now you need to be on the lookout for culture killers—the small (or not so small) things that can chip away at your culture and quickly become poisonous influences on morale. Here are some of the most common offenders and how to cut them off at the pass:

- **Focusing too much on a hierarchical organization.** One aspect of my leadership style is my preference for flatter organizations over highly hierarchical ones. Now don't get me wrong: I don't think that a totally flat organization is a good idea. Direct reporting structure is very important to provide clarity and accountability. But leaders who focus too strongly on the hierarchical model run the risk of implying that the importance of someone's voice and opinion is directly related to his or her rank on an organizational chart. That's not helpful in promoting collaboration, and it certainly does not encourage people to step up and use their voices to share new ideas.

When I think of leadership and management, these groups' primary role is to support the various teams, providing whatever guidance is needed to help them get their jobs done in the most efficient way possible. The leader–employee relationship is symbiotic in that each relies on the other to succeed; the employee may execute a task or project, but the leader needs to offer the strategy, the tools, and the power to remove any potential obstacles that may hinder the employee's work. This relationship is built on mutual trust and respect.

As for the old-school organizational chart, it does provide structure and sets expectations about responsibilities. But I think a firm that relies too heavily on a rigid structure can quickly become stagnant and hinder growth. I have seen and experienced a few situations in which the hierarchical approach means that your career is only as successful as the guy right above you thinks it should be. That's not the kind of culture that puts people first or aligns with heart leadership.

In my firms the organizational chart is used for reporting purposes and accountability, and from time to time to talk about how a project might be divided up and assigned. We've purposely focused on a flatter organization that does not put an emphasis on rank, titles, or who has the most direct reports.

That may be unnerving to some companies, but it really works for my firms to help build a sense of team. How? It promotes equality of voice and encourages collaboration. Now in the end, yes, there are bosses and no one forgets that. In many situations I do still need to make the ultimate decision. But that does not diminish any one individual's contributions to a project or an initiative.

- **Complacency.** Sharon Hoover, my executive coach and dear friend, once said to me that culture is what happens when you're not looking. Leadership and culture are not items on a list that can be checked off and completed. It's constantly looking left and right, paying attention to what's happening behind the scenes, and being sensitive to even the most glacial pace of discontent that may be settling into the workplace. Just because no one is screaming from the rafters to express their frustration and unhappiness does not mean everyone's satisfied. Once a leader takes any of this for granted, bad things can happen. Morale goes down. People feel stymied. They start looking for employment elsewhere. Sometimes the only communication you get from an employee who is unhappy is her resignation notice. It is vitally important to keep a keen sense of awareness of these things.

  Here's a recent example of how we managed to cut off a potential culture killer at the pass. We just had our first retirement at Private Ocean: our chief investment officer, who was never big on getting attention or on big parties in his honor. It would have been easy to let his departure slip by with maybe a card on his desk, but the last thing we wanted was for people to think that we would simply let a valuable member of our firm disappear without a show of appreciation. So during our usual lunch gathering with report-outs, we had a mini-celebration that was tailored to his style without making him feel uncomfortable. We wanted to be sure to send the message that the long career with the company prior to retirement was a *big deal*, and appreciated!

Fighting complacency with diligence is key to maintaining a happy and healthy workplace. If you've created a culture of open communication, remind your employees of this and encourage them to speak out. But don't sit back and wait for the phone to ring. Stop by offices, poke your head over cubicle walls, and take someone out to lunch. Ask questions, welcome feedback, and be open to change and advice. Don't ever think you have all the answers.

- **Not guiding the troops.** In a small firm, nobody has the luxury of wearing one hat. That does not mean we as employers get a pass on the proper mentoring of our employees. Have you set clear expectations for everyone in the office? If you asked each person what his job description is, (1) could he do it? and (2) how close is that description to his goals? A common mistake is leaders' assumption that because they have a mission statement, their staff members understand what role they play in delivering on that mission for clients. Overlooking this key component can lead to disappointment, frustration, and employee turnover, which in turn costs you time, money, and security in the future.

No matter what their roles are in your firm, all employees need guidance to grow and to help you build the business. Set expectations and standards for each role in your firm. Have clear job descriptions; in fact, employees could draft their own so that you can see if you and they are aligned in your expectations. During the hiring process, take to heart what a candidate's goals are, and once hired, apply them. Meet regularly with your team to make sure you both stay on the same page. Remember to think of your staff as your clients— take the time to get to know them and their needs.

All employees should have personal development plans. These plans should include their personal and professional goals and how they plan to achieve them. Employees can use them to set quarterly goals for themselves that are in alignment with the overall company goals. This structure is very effective in moving the company forward and inspiring employees.

- **Holding on to toxic employees.** You know the ones I am talking about. They have negative attitudes, they don't pull their weight—or worse, many times they have excellent skills yet others avoid them at all cost—and they just don't fit into your firm. Negativity in any environment, but especially in a small one, is as contagious as an airborne virus, affecting office morale, productivity, and your stress level. Why do we hold on to these employees? Maybe their skill set is impressive on paper, or maybe you're just avoiding unnecessary confrontation and hoping that it will work itself out.

Avoiding short-term pain in exchange for long-term pain is a nearsighted outlook that you will pay for in the end. What we don't consider is the cost. Think of your business as a living organism shaped like a wheel with spokes: As a living organism the life blood flows around the wheel and through the spokes. Imagine each spoke represents an employee. A toxic employee is like a blood clot! Work (flowing like blood) is inhibited and actually avoids the clot! The other employees work harder to compensate for the blood clot! Your business will not stop with one broken spoke or so-called blood clot, but the effects of everyone working around this person will start to wear on the firm.

The solution? Be frank and direct. Have a sit-down with this employee immediately and be honest about the issues and your desire to either correct the problem or part ways. Set very clear expectations about what is required from him. The sooner you do, the sooner your business, and your other employees, will thank you for it.

As an aside, I often say that a strong culture once created will stay true to itself. People will either assimilate, or, if they don't fit in, will find their way out. It takes everybody to promote and perpetuate that culture, and if it's healthy and strong enough, the culture will organically push the negative entities out. I have seen this happen in many cases at my firms, which means that the wrong employees don't last long and the right ones stick around through thick and thin.

Learning from your mistakes is worth its weight in gold, but learning from others' mistakes is priceless. These culture killers are insidious and can be costly to the firm if not kept in check!

Rolling Up Your Sleeves and Getting Involved

To begin your cultural evolution, you need to put a stake in the ground. Employees need to know that the times are changing, and here's why and how it's going to happen— and most important, here's what's in it for them! As with any change you are trying to create and promote, you *must* explain clearly the benefits to the employees for doing this.

If you want to promote a people-first culture, it sets a very clear tone for your employees if they feel as if they're shoulder-to-shoulder with their leaders. However, if you consistently put yourself above the team or stress the boundaries of rank and titles too much, you're doing yourself and your firm a disservice—not to mention missing out on some truly fulfilling experiences. Build bridges, not moats!

If creating events and spending more time with your team seems like a challenge at first, start small with some initiatives that encourage communication and personal interaction. Here are a few ideas we've used in Private Ocean to help foster a stronger culture:

- **Build an internal mentoring program.** Pair up senior advisors with junior advisors, and team leads or veteran employees with newer members. Give the program some structure—quarterly check-ins, shadowing exercises, goal planning—and make mentoring part of your employees' personal growth plans. I personally offer to meet with each advisor monthly for an hour to talk about anything she would like—how to handle client cases, advice on her education pursuits, and so on. It is a chance for me to mentor our advisors one-on-one.

- **Start a leadership book club.** At Private Ocean we have implemented the Leadership Book Club. Approximately three to four times per year a book (at first chosen by me but as time went on—to all of our benefit—also suggested by others) is read and then we have a discussion about the following: (1) Why was the book chosen? (2) What are the main takeaways of the book? (3) What can we implement personally or as a company to improve things at Private Ocean? Although these discussions are optional, everyone is encouraged to attend these sessions and the vast majority of the employees participate.

LEADERSHIP BOOKS TO CONSIDER

The 5 Essential People Skills, Dale Carnegie Training
Difficult Conversations, Douglas Stone, Bruce Patton,
  and Sheila Heen
The Heart of Mentoring, David Stoddard, with Robert
  Tamasy
Leadership and Self-Deception, The Arbinger Institute
Leadership by the Book, Ken Blanchard, Bill Hybels,
  and Phil Hodges
The Leadership Pill, Ken Blanchard and Marc Muchnick
Leading at a Higher Level, Ken Blanchard
Mindset, Carol S. Dweck

- **Encourage volunteer opportunities.** Volunteering
  to help your community is a great team-building exercise, but don't forget to recognize individual efforts. An
  event that our entire company participated in included
  packing groceries for a local charity. We appointed a
  small steering committee (which is another leadership
  training opportunity) to manage everything from planning to finances to materials. The effect on the entire
  team was a rewarding one, and it showcased the skills
  of some very capable team members.

Fostering leadership skills is rooted in practicing the
fundamentals of leadership. You'll find that these practical exercises, however big or small you choose to make
them, will help to build a culture of open communication,

collegiality, and inclusion that keeps employees motivated and the firm running smoothly.

A company's unique culture is ever evolving, just as your business is. And as with your business it takes everybody to support, nurture, and protect its culture to keep it healthy. A strong, happy work culture is a powerful tool that can boost morale, promote employee retention, and create a collaborative environment of great minds working together, leading to great company success. But it's also incredibly fragile. It's never perfect, and it will always require your attention.

My leadership style may not be conventional, but it has carved out for me a unique path toward success and growth—both personally and professionally. By combining the lessons I have learned from my past with these seven elements of heart leadership, I have created a fulfilling outlet to realize my vision and priority of focusing on people. And though my approach may have evolved over time to meet the needs of my employees and my clients, at its core these values have never wavered. My commitment to serving others and helping them grow is genuine and unwavering—and something my team members know they can always rely on.

As a leader trying to navigate changing times, I encourage you to take that first step toward building a culture that is rewarding to both your people and to the health and future of your firm. All it really takes is caring—and to remember those basic principles of human nature that we teach our children: patience, honesty and integrity, compassion, respect, persistence and consistency, encouragement, and courage.

I often quote my executive coach, Sharon Hoover, when I say that culture trumps strategy every time, and it's true. You simply cannot go wrong when you lead with your heart and let your actions follow.

Courage Recap: Tips to Remember

- Look inward. What kind of leader do you perceive yourself to be and what kind of leader are you striving to be?
- Consider the use of an executive coach.
- Look at your company and its current culture. Ask yourself:
  - What is your personal idea of a fulfilling work culture?
  - What things matter most to you in your career?
  - Are you surrounded by the kinds of people who would support you and join you in this endeavor?
  - Do their goals align with yours?
- Identify all culture killers and how you can overcome them.
- Don't be afraid to get involved and create change! Culture starts and ends at the top.

Benefits

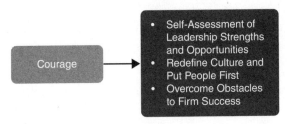

Note

1. Sharon Birkman Fink and Stephanie Capparell, *The Birkman Method: Your Personality at Work* (San Francisco: Jossey-Bass, 2013).

Chapter 8

Implementing Heart Culture in Your Firm

Get Started Today, Not Tomorrow

A sk people to describe a great business leader and chances are you will get a wide, varied list of attributes. Some will say that truly great leaders are also great listeners, or that they are diplomatic, considerate, and fair. Others will say that great leaders should be innovative, confident, and fearless. Nobody is wrong, really. The truth is great leaders can be any of these things, but what they should all have in common is *heart*. This is certainly not to say that there aren't other forms of leadership that have been tremendously successful (if success is defined in terms of growth and finances) that would certainly not be characterized as caring about people—and

while this is true, there are *many* more examples of successful companies where heart is at the core!

My approach to leadership has always been focused on
cultivating a culture based on the most basic of human
values. These values are seeded deep within us as we strive
to do good, be better people, and find ways to live fulfilling
personal and professional lives. Holding on to those values
in the workplace helps cultivate a very centered and grati-
fying corporate culture. A culture that centers on what the
heart wants first.

And what does the heart want? It's simple, really.
Happiness. People want to feel that they make a difference,
that their efforts *matter.* As a leader, I want happy employees
who come to work in a healthy, happy environment with
people they respect and admire. I want clients who experience that happiness and feel that our firm's priorities align
with theirs. That's why I share my vision of a successful,
collaborative, and inspirational culture with every single
new hire. I then ask for that employee's own personal goals
for achieving happiness. The response I get usually helps
determine if that person will fit into our culture or is des-
tined to move on. Keeping the right people in and letting
the wrong people go is key to maintaining the integrity of
your firm's culture.

So now that you've been introduced to the Seven Steps
of Heart Culture and have seen how all of the pieces fit
together, it's time to get started.

What can you do to put your firm on the path to heart
culture? It may seem daunting but the challenges are more
than worth the rewards to your business and to you, both
as a leader and a person.

1. **Decide that you want to make a change.** That means tapping into your own personal desires for happiness (and how you *define* happiness) and how your aspirations can translate to your firm.

2. **Start talking.** Engage an executive coach and get an assessment of your current culture. Talk to your employees about what drives them to succeed. Ask them who inspires them and what their goals are for the future.

3. **Draw up a plan.** No one says you have to change the world in a day, but you do have to take action. That may mean holding round-table discussions with employees about their needs and their frustrations. It could involve a company retreat to communicate your visions for the firm's future. When your employees see that you're actively changing the course of communication, you'll hear more voices speak up than you expected.

4. **Never let up on the momentum.** Maintaining what you start is as important as deciding to make a change. If you decide to hold weekly lunch-and-learn sessions to help employees meet with leadership, you have to keep those going, or replace them with something equally beneficial to your employees.

Many advisors—including myself—would say that they got into the financial services industry because they wanted to help people, and that the service they provide is their contribution to society. I got into the wealth management business because I wanted to help people live better lives, achieve their financial and life goals, and not outlive their money.

Our *job* is to care, but I believe that no matter the industry, we are all innate heart leaders by nature.

I have heard—and wholeheartedly believe—that culture trumps strategy every time. Why? Because no matter how well-meaning a leader is in trying to strategize for success through development plans and forecasts, it's the right *culture* that actually makes things happen. Simply put, a great culture that is positive, inspiring, supportive, and collaborative improves execution—and can help your staff climb mountains!

Leading with heart and striving to provide a caring culture for your employees is not only beneficial for your firm's success, it also reminds us that at our core we are all people working together toward a common goal. That unique experience you are able to deliver to your team— camaraderie, honest communication, collaboration—is not only potent, it can live on far beyond an employee's tenure in your firm.

The most precious thing about heart culture isn't its impact on a company's success but rather that the movement is contagious. And with the right nurturing and growth, it can stay with someone throughout their future. Even for a lifetime.

Taking that first step toward a culture change could make the biggest difference in your firm and also greatly impact those who depend on you. The power to make that change is within us all, so all it takes is to decide to do what comes naturally.

To lead with our hearts.

Afterword

When I met Greg Friedman early in 2001, he already understood the value of having an executive coach. He'd worked with several to help with his own growth previously, and was now looking for someone to facilitate a retreat for Friedman & Associates. But before I met his team Greg wanted the two of us to work together and build a relationship that would allow me to look from the outside in at how he ran his business and to give him unbiased feedback. He was—and is—very thoughtful and paid great care to due diligence. We spent three months working together before his retreat to get to know each other, and this gave me great insight into who he was as a leader and as a person.

That first retreat included a small group of people, and in all honesty I felt a little (expected) apprehension from the group. It's always a bit strange to have someone at a company event who is not really part of the team.

But Greg quickly set the tone that I was there to help, not critique, how the firm was doing. We got on really well that first time out, and years afterward people became more and more comfortable with me, even making me feel like one of the gang. That easy camaraderie is part of how Greg makes people feel included, and it is really a testament to how well he chooses the right people for his team.

At Junxure, Greg brought me in very early to help facilitate its company retreats. There were maybe six or so people back then, and Greg was really focused on how he could run two businesses at once successfully and fairly. This was no easy feat, but no matter the obstacles, Greg always faced each day the same way. His attitude was always that he would do whatever it took to be successful and to provide a healthy, happy work environment for his people.

The culture at both Private Ocean and Junxure is the same now as it was then because of Greg's passion and commitment to their people. He is acutely aware that culture starts and ends at the top, and he also understands that there is no best culture, only what works best for the people involved. Greg has put together a group of people who he truly cares about, who share common goals and who have a similar outlook on life and happiness. None of that was a coincidence.

Greg knows that the key to business success is its people. Simply put, you don't succeed without your people, and retaining good people is what helps the company grow.

Not everyone is a good cultural fit for his firms, and that's okay. Greg recognizes that searching for the right person means an investment of time up front that will pay dividends in the long run.

I have tremendous respect for Greg, not only for his dedication to his people but also for his openness to change and to coaching. An often-overlooked key asset to being an excellent leader is the ability to acknowledge not having all the answers. Rather than viewing this as a vulnerability, an effective leader is always open to what someone else sees in him and is receptive to considering how that information can be of use to him. Greg has never shied away from feedback—from his employees or his clients—and that has helped him build his reputation in the industry.

Anyone who has met Greg knows he is truly one of a kind. He is honest, available, and generous. He does not hide his feelings. What you see with Greg is what you get, and in the corporate world—no matter the industry—that kind of openness is refreshing. It helps him connect with people in any setting, and he runs his business with that same positive expression. The culture he and his team have built together has come from who he is as a person. These people care for one another. They deflect praise in favor of promoting their teammates. They work together no matter the obstacles and do it with pride and personal satisfaction.

Culture is something that Greg understands is key to building and sustaining a lasting, successful business. Knowing him as I do after these 14-plus years, it makes perfect sense that he would now want to share his insight with other leaders who may be struggling or who may simply want to improve on what they've started. I look forward to seeing what the future has in store for him and his people as they continue to take on the world together.

Sharon Hoover, Coaching Works

References

Birkman Fink, Sharon, and Stephanie Capparell. 2013. *The Birkman Method: Your Personality at Work*. San Francisco: Jossey-Bass.

Lencioni, Patrick. 2010. *Getting Naked: A Business Fable about Shedding the Three Fears That Sabotage Client Loyalty*. San Francisco: Jossey-Bass.

Mamet, David. 1994. *Glengarry Glen Ross*, reissue edition. New York: Grove Press.

Mehrabian, Albert, and Morton Wiener. 1967. "Decoding of Inconsistent Communications." *Journal of Personality and Social Psychology* 6 (1): 109–114. doi:10.1037/h0024532. PMID 6032751.

Mehrabian, Albert, and Susan R. Ferris. 1967. "Inference of Attitudes from Nonverbal Communication in Two Channels." *Journal of Consulting Psychology* 31 (3): 248–252. doi:10.1037/h0024648.

Nelson, Noelle C. 2012. *Make More Money by Making Your Employees Happy*. Malibu, CA: MindLab Publishing.

Pfeffer, Jeffrey. 1998. *The Human Equation: Building Profits by Putting People First*. Boston: Harvard Business Review Press.

Pfeffer, Jeffrey, and John F. Veiga. 1999. "Putting People First for Organizational Success." *Academy of Management Executive* 13 (2): 37–48.

Sirota, David, and Douglas A. Klein. 2013. *The Enthusiastic Employee: How Companies Profit by Giving Workers What They Want*, 2nd ed. Upper Saddle River, NJ: Pearson Education.

Wolters Kluwer, CCH. 2007. *Unscheduled Absence Survey*. Riverwoods, IL: Wolters Kluwer, CCH.

About the Author

Gregory H. Friedman, MS, CFP®, is founder and president of both Junxure and Private Ocean. Junxure is a practice-improvement firm that integrates software, training, and consulting to help advisors streamline operations, deliver exceptional client service, and grow their practices intelligently. Private Ocean is one of the West Coast's leading wealth management firms.

Greg is a relentless innovator and advocate for excellent wealth management. He is widely recognized as one of the nation's top financial advisors. *Investment Advisor* magazine included Greg three times on its list of the top 25 most influential financial advisors. He was named one of six 2011 Industry Influencers by *Financial Planning* magazine, an award presented to six advisors "whose innovative ideas and wide-reaching work are forging new paths for the planning industry." In 2008, Charles Schwab Institutional presented Greg's previous firm, Friedman & Associates, with its prestigious IMPACT Award for Best in Tech.

Greg is a frequent speaker at industry conferences on a wide range of topics, including practice management, mergers, succession, technology, and building a successful wealth management business.

Index